ADVENTURES *in* LIVING

ADVENTURES *in* LIVING

From Cato to George Sand

By
MURIEL JAEGER

Essay Index Reprint Series

 BOOKS FOR LIBRARIES PRESS
FREEPORT, NEW YORK

First Published 1932
Reprinted 1970

LIBRARY
FLORIDA STATE UNIVERSITY
TALLAHASSEE, FLORIDA

INTERNATIONAL STANDARD BOOK NUMBER:
0-8369-1758-8

LIBRARY OF CONGRESS CATALOG CARD NUMBER:
79-121480

PRINTED IN THE UNITED STATES OF AMERICA

CONTENTS

		PAGE
	INTRODUCTION	V
I	THE STOIC	1
II	THE CHRISTIAN	44
III	THE MAN OF THE WORLD	89
IV	THE CHILD OF NATURE	135
V	THE FREE WOMAN	170

INTRODUCTION

Most men, with whatever ideas they may start out in youth, resign themselves in the end to living as circumstances demand of them. A very few, of tougher fibre, try to live according to plan. Usually, these are not the most attractive individuals, and very often they do a great deal of harm. None the less, experiments in conduct are far from being the least interesting and useful of experiments. The sufferings of Tolstoy's wife make one of the world's tragedies, but they have to be balanced against what Tolstoy's experiences have added to the interest and significance of life for the elect thousands who are concerned with the moral possibilities of human nature.

Such experiments in conduct invariably fail at some point, and perhaps always will fail, since, in spite of the speculations of our Utopian thinkers, man seems unlikely ever to attain complete control over his environment. Accordingly, small, hard, incompatible facts crop up. The spiritual athlete trips over an irrelevant tuft and becomes a sprawling joke for the crowd to laugh at. He may take it in a sporting spirit, like the Buddha when he admitted that he had found he could not contemplate really well on an empty stomach. Or he may take it hardly, like Nietzsche, who said that the greatness of a soul was measured by the load of morbidity that it could carry, yet found his own load too heavy for his sanity. But, whatever the fate of the experimenter in conduct, he leaves behind for his fellow-men food for thought; and a man who does this can hardly be said to have lived an entirely futile life.

VI

Coherent schemes of human behaviour can be brought under a very few heads. Let us adopt a strict code of morality, and keep up a running fight against everything that conflicts with it; let us be completely altruistic; let us accept society as it stands, learn to manipulate it like an artist, and be the completely civilised man; let us revert to primitive simplicity; let us trust our impulses of the moment and follow wherever they may lead. These attitudes almost cover those possible to thinking men in any age or society. One is missing, that of the withdrawal, the Buddha's solution; but perhaps no Western mind can fully understand that enterprise.

The individuals who have succeeded in carrying out such dominating ideas with any approach to consistency are also very few. It is a rôle that requires very special qualifications. Both creative imagination and iron resolution are necessary to the artist in conduct, and besides these, he needs, like other artists, limitations as well as capacities – in particular, a gift for ignoring paradox. Moreover, he will hardly get far unless he possesses, in the first place, a position of advantage in society, so that he has, at least, some initial control over circumstances. It will usually be found that the personalities whose conduct of life has become a legend, were aristocrats in the early ages of the world, and, at least, wealthy middle-class in more recent centuries. St. Francis's embrace of Lady Poverty would hardly have made the sensation that it did if it had been necessary. George Sand could not have passed so freely from lover to lover if her literary gift had not enabled her to support them. Even the Simple-Lifer, Thomas Day, found the Simple Life expensive, and would hardly have been able to live it at all if his father had not left him a private income. Also, until recently, such figures have always been men; the handicap on women in the earlier phases of society must have been too severe. Saint Clare could be almost as poor as Saint Francis, but she had to have somewhere to live and could not roam about the roads of Italy practising universal brotherhood. Aphra Behn could break loose from convention, but she could not also ignore the conventions of unconventionality and practise free love without promiscuity. All our experimenters, therefore, are inevitably people of some position in the world and all but the most recent belong to the privileged sex. Perhaps there have also been poor men and obscure women who have tried to live a theory, but, if so, we have never heard of them, or too little for the experiment to be illuminating.

With all their advantages, our experimenters in conduct found sufficient difficulty. Apart from the perversity of the outside world, human nature is the most intractable medium of all, and these intrepid pioneers had not only the human nature of other men to deal with, but also their own. It is hardly surprising that most of them at some point retreated into the more manageable world of literature. Another contrary danger also beset them. Inevitably, they had audiences. They were thus doomed to self-consciousness and, in the end, to self-parody. To know what is expected of one and still to behave independently is perhaps beyond the possibilities of human will-power.

The personalities studied in the following essays were all, from one point of view, failures. Taking their difficulties into account, they were surprising successes. Even in success, they appear more or less ridiculous, for laughter is Nature's check on the human being who tries in any way to transcend her. We, in the present age, can afford to laugh at them, because we do not aim so high.

VIII

Our age, in the moral sphere, is the child who knocks down towers, not the child who builds them. Still, it may be worth our while to take another glance at some of these odd structures before we demolish them. We may yet do worse. Some future student of experiments in conduct may yet find among our own contemporaries a more ludicrous figure even than the Free Woman, or the Simple-Lifer. He will probably call it 'The Complete Opportunist.'

I

THE STOIC

MOST of us have come across the young man who is the starting-point of our first study. He is usually very young indeed, in his late 'teens or early twenties. He is a disconcerting youth with steady, grave, innocent eyes who regards with a puzzled surprise many of our quite harmless little ways. For his own part, his habits are above reproach. He dresses plainly and without pandering to climatic vagaries. He is abstemious at his meals and disdains the sociable minor vices. He wears no hat in sun or rain; he will habitually refuse a lift, preferring to go on foot. He distresses his relatives by appearing at social functions, if at all, in a costume suitable to a camping holiday. If an honour is awarded to him which he feels he has not fairly earned, he will embarrass the donors by refusing it. If a friend asks him to use his 'pull' to obtain him a job or an advantage, the reply will probably involve the end of the friendship. If he comes into the independent income of which we could ourselves make such excellent use, he celebrates the occasion by reducing his expenditure. He is likely, if he is old enough, to be engaged in some form of public work, and he will always be the first to arrive and the last to go at his office. Like Pompey, when he received a visit from such a young man in Asia, people 'honour him when he is present and are glad when he goes away.'

Most of us have not only met him, but have at one time passed through a similar phase ourselves – that uncomfortable priggish phase of cold baths, early morning runs, no smoking, and complete incomprehension why everyone does not always behave as he ought. But, long ago, of course, we have grown, or shrunk, out of it. To maturity, it is a ludicrous phase. The silly child has no idea what the world is like; he thinks he can make it over again to his own plans of what is right and fitting. He has not yet faced the savage competition of his fellow-men; he doesn't know that he must use every advantage he can get, or go under; that the law and public opinion are the only limiting influences that those who mean to do something with their lives can afford to admit. If we once had similar ideas ourselves, we have the less tolerance for him, because, in that case, he is a living reproach to the younger self which perhaps still lingers on in us somewhere. The French, with their genius for ironic dismissal, label him *'très socialiste'* and leave him to come to his senses; and we are all of us glad to know that he will soon have all that nonsense hammered out of him and become a reasonable, companionable person with whom one can share a mildly salacious story over a glass and a cigarette. Young Cato, about to go to Asia on the visit which so disconcerted Pompey, was told by his friend Curio, that he would bring back 'a better temper and pleasanter manners.'

It was not, perhaps, the best way to influence a youth in the direction of greater adaptability. Young people of character are apt to be contra-suggestible to the supercilious prophecies of their elders. Cato, fêted in Asia, told his companions to watch well and look after him, lest he should end by making good Curio's words. One suspects, however, that the danger was never very great. What Cato was in his early twenties he remained throughout a life of forty-nine years and died in maintaining.

The achievement is a problem in human nature. At no time could it have been easy, perhaps at no other time would it have been possible. Among ourselves, for instance, one cannot imagine a young man of intelligence above the average keeping it up for more than a year or two. The futility of it would be too plainly forced upon him. He would find himself merely a bull to be baited. It would not be a question simply of the hostility of his fellows or even of persecution, but of the deadliest enemy of all – ridicule. But then, with us, morality is out of fashion, not only in practice, but in theory. In the Rome of Cato's time it was rapidly becoming out of fashion in practice, but not yet in theory. Cato's race was still the one that idealised a father who had condemned his son to death for winning a battle contrary to orders, whose greatest generals passed from leading an army to driving a plough and whose typical hero went back to death by torture among enemies, because he had pledged his word. Cato's contemporaries, when they saw him performing similar feats, felt the same half proud, half amused recognition as we feel for the few 'old English gentlemen' – hearty drinkers, hard riders, paternal landlords – who are still to be found among us.

In fact, morality has become, for us, a dull subject. It is a bold writer or speaker who now uses the word 'virtue' in a sympathetic sense at all. Not that we are any the less ready to say that people 'ought' or 'ought not' to do this and that and the other, but that we are weary and sceptical of universal 'musts.' It is not easy to remember that codes of right conduct were once just as much new toys as wireless telephony or Freudian psychology are now. Living, as we do, at the end of millenniums of civilization – or, at least, of such civilization as comes from written records of the past – of a knowledge of what men have thought and decided since abstract thought became possible, we are liable to forget that there must have been a phase in human development when this, too, was pioneering work, when the suggestion of a principle of conduct was as interesting as the discovery of radium. Our intransigeant young Roman did not live in the first freshness of man's discovery of himself as a conscious being – that had been the happiness of the Greeks of the age of Socrates – but he lived when the discovery had just touched his own race and it was possible to feel 'that who could see Virtue would be wonderfully ravished with the love of her beauty.'

In the Rome of Cato's time, philosophy (and more especially the moral side of it) was very much in fashion. Most men, of course, kept it sensibly in a water-tight compartment, just as our enthusiastic psychologists usually carry on comfortably enough with the ordinary human sentiments and spites and jealousies. Only a few, like Cicero, who had the fatal yearning of the intellectual man after consistency, made spasmodic efforts to apply it, sometimes bringing their conduct into line with their theory, sometimes trying to twist the theory to fit their conduct. But no one with any pretensions to culture could laugh freely at the man who seriously tried to apply his philosophy.

It was fortunate for the early philosophers that they knew less than we know now about human limitations. The discovery of our times is the re-discovery that we are animals; the discovery of the ancients was that they were men. The brilliance of such new lights temporarily obscures other equally important ones. Abstract thought is discredited with us – what can it do against the old instincts and appetites, against the voracious brute, hardly curbed by fear, that ramps in each of us? For them, abstract thought was the king and master, the supremely human quality. There was nothing, they believed, that it could not do. All ancient systems of philosophy are based on the assumption that what one can conceive intellectually one can carry out in practice. You had merely to discover the principles of right conduct, and you became master of your fate – the sage, the 'blessed man.' Since outside circumstances obviously could not always be controlled, it followed that they were irrelevant. It was not an arrogant Stoic, but Epicurus himself, the apostle of 'Pleasure' as the highest good, who claimed that the wise man would be happy even while he was being burnt alive.

The Stoics, who chose 'moral worth' as the final good, insisted that happiness went with it. It is hardly necessary to define the ingredients of 'moral worth' – they were those principles of conduct that naturally recommended themselves to our admirable priggish youth. To the Stoic they appeared, in fact, 'natural' – one of the most slippery words in the dictionary and no less so in its Greek and Latin equivalents. In ancient usage, it perhaps most nearly approaches the quality that we should describe as 'rational.' It was, to them, natural that men should be rational. 'To rob your neighbour or to make profit at another's expense is more contrary to nature,' wrote Cicero, 'than death, want, pain or any bodily or external misfortune.' 'Injustice is fatal to human fellowship and society,' while 'the mental assent to what is false, as the Stoics believe, is more repugnant to us than all the other things that are contrary to nature.'

The Stoic slogan was the password given by the dying emperor, Antoninus Pius, *aequanimitas*. A true Stoic, not only ought to be, but, in the nature of things, must be, absolutely unaffected by pain, misfortune, disease or unruly emotion. Outside circumstances were indifferent to him and defeat in the practical sphere was of no importance. 'All wise men at all times enjoy a happy, perfect and fortunate life free from all hindrance, interference or want.' 'It is no use, pain,' said Posidonius, carrying on a philosophic conversation in the midst of an attack of gout, 'for all the distress you cause, I shall never admit that you are an evil.' Unfortunately even Stoic philosophers had sometimes a stronger sense of actuality. One of them was convinced by a bout of kidney trouble that pain was not entirely irrelevant to the 'blessed life.' 'If I, who have spent many years in studying philosophy, am unable to bear pain,' he announced, 'pain must be an evil.' 'A person of little resolution,' is Cicero's contemptuous comment.

Like all logical systems that have to do with human nature, Stoicism can in fact soon be brought to paradox and absurdity. None the less, this feeling that we must in some way make ourselves independent of circumstances is perennial. If a man behaves well, nothing can really touch him ; probably every intelligent human being has a strong impulse to that belief, whatever his standard of good behaviour may be – Stoicism, Christianity or sportsmanship. And yet it so obviously does not always pay to behave well. Not only is virtue often its own and only reward, but it is common experience that people frequently suffer more for their virtues than for their faults. Most religions escape that hard fact by supplying mystic compensations, consoling visions, sense of unity with the Infinite, or, more prosaically, a really solid happiness in a future life, with music, gardens, feasting and houris. Stoicism has been the only religion which insisted that 'moral worth' must and did pay in itself, adequately and on the nail. There is, after all, a certain glamour in such naked defiance of what life can do to one. Our naturally defiant youth in the Rome of the first century B.C. found this naturally defiant religion waiting for him.

The Rome of the first century B.C. was, however, in other respects sufficiently like other places and times to supply a tough and resistant medium for the creation of the righteous life. Cato was practically born a public man, and politics are the same the world over. At Rome, at that moment, they were particularly vivid and typical in that circumstances had intensified to the highest degree the struggle of old against new. The city state was becoming an empire with alarming rapidity, and its institutions, developed to suit the necessities of a small, concentrated, easily manipulated community, were cracking under the strain. Its citizens were intoxicated by new possibilities – possibilities of great wealth, great power, extreme luxury. Other things than philosophy had come from Greece, aesthetic interests and refinements, an atmosphere of mental subtlety such as works like a rot on more primitive natures. A Roman among Greeks found himself in much the same helpless confusion as Bernard Shaw's simple stockbroker in Heartbreak House. One could not pin a Greek down; he was off up a tree while one was still getting into position; he questioned everything, turned arguments upside down and inside out, made black appear white; effecting breath-taking transvaluations, so that all that one had thought most solid and certain dissolved in mists of scepticism.

The Romans of Cato's time were already becoming a little acclimatized to the new conditions. Culture had become possible to the upper classes; unscrupulousness not only possible, but rampant. Big bosses were taking charge of the new forces which the old institutions were quite unable to handle. The republican machinery, in fact, was laughable in its extreme unwieldiness. There were twenty chief magistrates, replaced every year. Each of them had the power to make decrees having the force of law; most of them could exercise a veto on any decree of any of the others. There was, accordingly, nothing that any man with influence could not have done, or have stopped, for anyone could buy at least one of these chief magistrates if he had the means. The only real limitation was public opinion and that, too, could now usually be bought. Cicero remarks that the rate of interest for ready money rose from four to six per cent. during the July elections. The senate, now an advisory body of ex-officials, had also a genuine influence, since it was permanent and vocal. And tradition was still strong enough to exercise some restraint. When Caesar had Cato arrested on one occasion, the senate arose in a body and accompanied him and his gaolers, and Caesar was embarrassed into finding a magistrate to veto his own action.

Such Gilbertian situations were becoming common in Roman politics. The idea of 'Sovereignty' – that there must be some final authority which could effect and overrule anything whatever, was not understood – was in fact, partly the outcome of these very difficulties. It is strange that, after all, even in modern times, self-locking machinery in government still exists, so that the free people of the United States, having got in their eighteenth amendment, cannot get it out again and disobey their own law instead. Such situations are the paradoxical result of over-careful safeguarding of liberties. In modern England, on the other hand, the 'King in Parliament' can at any time do anything whatever that may be necessary – alter any law, condemn any citizen to death, reduce the value of the currency – in a day's session. But only in desperate emergency could the Romans appoint a dictator or give the consuls plenary powers. In their case, too, it was the meticulous safeguarding of liberty, the careful division of power, resulting from social struggles between the Patricians and the Plebeians through many centuries, that had produced a government so singularly unfitted to deal with a scattered, growing empire where rapid and final decisions were vital. It was the Big Boss's ideal opportunity.

And yet it was still a great thing to be what Cato was – a Roman patrician. One had a dignified life from the earliest years; slaves did all the dirty work; if one was trained to have a hard body and a hard mind, it was from choice, not from necessity. One lived half freely, half decorously, much in the open air and sun, often in the country. In town, in the friendly Italian climate, it was still an open-air life in the sociability of the streets, the baths and the forum. As a boy, one studied under a tutor or in a small school among equals, learning especially the art of impressive oratory, taking part in free and ritual sports with one's contemporaries, and conscious always of a destined importance. At about fifteen, one formally put on the *toga virilis* and was a grown man. In later years, one would wear the praetor's robe with the purple border and give judgment in the courts. In early middle life, one would be consul; everyone would stand when one passed, one's body would be sacred, and one's word, law. As pro-consul one would rule a province and lead great armies to victory, hear the shouting of the soldiers hailing one, 'Imperator!' and enter Rome in a Triumph with captives and spoils following in procession. From the time when one reached the early thirties, one would be a senator, a member of the body which Pyrrhus's envoy had called 'An Assembly of Kings,' giving views and votes on the destiny of nations. Life moved with a dramatic dignity, an impressive symbolism, such is now to be found only in the process of the Law. Moral strength was guarded and guided by magnificent phrases – the poetry of the Romans, whose *Morituri te salutamus* gives more poignantly the spirit of a race than all the pages of Virgil. It is the imposing obverse of that queer lack of humour which more complex peoples still find in the Italian.

So it had been, and so, in outward appearance, it still remained, though, actually, Greece and humour had already conquered. The magistrate still wore his *toga praetexta* over his venal body and soul; augurs declared the omens – good or bad, as it suited their bosses. Proconsuls still led armies to victory, though they were more interested in skinning the provincials. Senators gave forth rounded periods of patriotic oratory, exchanging cynical comments behind their hands. The outward shell of official dignity still remained, merely because no one quite knew how strong it still might be, nor what might not come down with it when it came down. One would not yet strike a consul, though one might buy him.

As for the young men, the coming senators and consuls and governors, Cicero describes their behaviour at a political crisis. 'A crowd of our dandies with their chin-tufts assembled, all the Catiline set, with Curio's girlish son at their head, and implored the people to reject it . . . Clodius's hired ruffians had filled up the entrances to the voting-boxes. The voting tickets were so manipulated that no "ayes" were distributed . . . Clodius threw himself at the feet of the Senators one after the other.'

Into this complicated game of bluff and chicanery walked our grave young man with all the prestige of a patrician and a practising Stoic, among men prepared to be variously admiring, amused, humiliated, exasperated, opportunist over him. They already knew something of what they had to expect. In Cato's family, the old tradition was at its stongest. His ancestors for many generations back had been distinguished men. His great-grandfather, Cato the Censor, had himself become a legend of integrity. Even as a small child, Cato had had the opportunity of defying a suitor to his uncle who humorously threatened to throw him out of a window if he would not 'use his influence' for him. At fourteen, he had offered to kill Sulla, the current 'big boss,' while he sat upon a couch with him, and was anxiously watched by his tutor, who already had reason to know the uncommonly close association between word and action in his pupil. The Roman aristocracy was a small, gossiping circle. Such incidents were passed round and discussed. Everyone knew that the latest Cato was showing himself 'a chip of the old block.'

Cato had thus grown up in the limelight. He made his first public speech while still a youngster in his 'teens on the occasion of a proposed alteration in a public building which his famous ancestor had given to the city. 'It had nothing youthful or refined in it,' says Plutarch, 'but was straightforward, full of matter and rough. At the same time there was a certain grace about his rough statements which won the attention, and the speaker's character, showing itself in all he said, added something to his severe language that excited feelings of natural pleasure and interest. His voice was full and sounding, sufficient to be heard by so great a multitude.' He won his point.

If one is determined to live according to certain standards, it is certainly a help to have that character established in the public eye. Cato's personality was defined before he was twenty. He would already have found it difficult to act out of that character if he had wished. Already, he was an artist who had found his public.

Cato's military service passed without opportunity for distinction except at its close, when he refused all marks of honour because he had not earned them. Following the usual routine, he then became a quaestor, a junior treasury official, and immediately an icy wind began to blow through the comfortable give-and-take atmosphere of Roman political life. Not much was expected – or wanted – of these young men passing year by year through the first formal stages of a political career. They had their small perquisites, their opportunities to give and receive favours. Business was carried on by the permanent officials. Cato at once upset the tradition by insisting on putting in a full day's work. This might have passed as a harmless eccentricity, if he had merely done what he was told; but his appalled colleagues soon found that he knew as much as they did about the business – or more. He had actually studied it beforehand and had a tactless understanding of all its details. The young Stoic turned his clear, innocent eyes upon Roman finance much as Hercules must have looked at the Augean stables, and then, like Hercules, plunged in. Many of the minor officials lost their jobs; people who owed the State money and had been well content to go on owing it, had to produce it quickly; State creditors who had cut their losses in despair suddenly found themselves paid in full. Senators began to find Cato's name useful when they wanted to put off importunate suitors. It was a terrible year for the wire-pullers and, even when it was over, the mischief was not done with. He kept slaves permanently at the office with orders to report all transactions to him. Ever afterwards one could never be sure what damaging facts might or might not be in his possession.

From his quaestorship, Cato passed into the 'Assembly of Kings' much as a large and vigorous wasp hurtles into a spider's web, and with very similar results. The sticky, delicate threads of intrigue and corruption wove and re-wove about him, were broken, and tirelessly spun again.

The old order was changing with the relentlessness of a natural phenomenon. It might have been guided, it could not be stopped. The righteous man's one chance would have been to form a party. There was probably still enough honesty, enough enthusiasm for the old traditions, to enable the right man, the man who could have used the necessary tools, to fight the big bosses before it was too late. It was, in many ways, an auspicious moment. Pompey, the biggest boss of all, was away in Asia, fighting and enriching himself, and Asia was then two thousand miles away – that is, two thousand miles of riding and running and sailing in small boats dependent on the wind and the rower, not two days' hop in an aeroplane or a few seconds by wireless telegraph. So that Pompey was very thoroughly out of the way. Only small wire-pullers, who might have been played off one against the other, remained in Rome. They had no unity of purpose and a small phalanx of the moderately well-intentioned could have operated with powerful effect.

But the completely righteous man is alone. No one but Cato was good enough for Cato's party. It was a party in which there could be no rewards, no compromises, no bargains, even no compliments. The end never justified the means. A man supported warmly by Cato one day would find himself knocked down by him the next. Not without a reason, certainly; there was always a very definite reason, a reason that could be, and usually was, publicly stated. But the persons concerned did not love him any the better on that account. They rubbed their bruises and scowled; or, if they were men of the world, they rubbed them and laughed. In either case, they looked elsewhere.

Another young man was entering politics at the same moment as Cato, a young man to whom facts were more important than principles. His manners were urbane, his behaviour friendly, his intentions not obtruded. He was popular, and he spent money freely, both openly and secretly. The Catiline conspiracy broke out before he was ready. It was an enterprise characteristic of the times. There was no principle behind it – it was merely that a group of lawless and dissipated young men wanted the appointments out of their turn, since one had to be a magistrate before one could have a province and a glorious opportunity for enriching oneself. It was later, when Catiline raised the countryside, that the movement almost took the form of a Peasants' Revolt, drawing in swarms of unemployed ex-soldiers and small-owners driven off the huge estates that were now worked by slave labour.

Cicero, an older man than Cato or Julius Caesar, was consul at the time. Here was another who, with a little more decision of character, might have headed the small party of decent men that might have saved republican Rome. He was a man of intellect and culture, a philosopher holding the principles of the New Academy – which, on the moral side, were a watered Stoicism. He was a lawyer, and, from a middle-class origin, had risen by his skill in advocacy. Unfortunately, he could never forget that middle-class origin, but remained through life the clever grammar-school lad among public-school boys. He was apologetic, boastful, greedy for praise and honours; he could not take hard knocks. Where his own position was concerned he lost all sense of proportion. His relations with Cato make a tragi-comedy.

They began, however, hopefully in the Catiline conspiracy. One of Cicero's secret agents discovered the plot, which included his own murder. In a corner, with his own life in danger, a timid man can sometimes act decisively. He demanded and obtained plenary powers from the senate, over-riding for the moment the stultifying veto system. Catiline himself had escaped into the country, but all the other conspirators were arrested. The Senate was called to decide what was to be done with them.

In the Senate-house, the young Stoic and the young opportunist Julius Caesar faced each other, dwarfing everyone else. There was a general intuition that Caesar had had an understanding with Catiline – a whisper that Cicero, in this one case, had suppressed the evidence; for already everyone believed that, if Caesar were touched, the people would rise. The thing must not be mentioned and, if Caesar himself were discreet, as he could be trusted to be, it might all blow over in safety. Within the limits of this discretion, he did what he could for his friends – they might yet be useful. Confiscation and banishment, he suggested, was the correct punishment for Roman patricians in such a case. It would be beneath the dignity of the Senate to be rushed by panic into the injustice of giving the death penalty. The speech, as quoted by Sallust, is such patent sophistry, that everyone must have seen through it. No doubt, Caesar cared nothing whether they did or not; he was relying on other forces, while, with his usual good manners, he gave the Senate a chance to save their faces.

Into this delicate situation, charged the other young man. They were discussing, he pointed out, how to punish men who intended to ruin their country, their families, their property and their religion. They could talk about fine points of legality when they had saved the city. Of course, he knew well enough that what they valued was their fine houses, fat incomes, pictures and trappings; but these would go with the rest, unless they could bring themselves to show a little resolution, even now at the eleventh hour. Caesar had made a smart speech in favour of a punishment that could at any moment be reversed. If Caesar did not fear the return of the conspirators then there was the more reason for the rest of them to fear it.

Perhaps it was at this point that a note was brought in to Caesar. Cato demanded that it should be read aloud. The urbane young man politely rose and handed it to him. It was a compromising letter from Cato's own sister, Servilia. Cato glanced at it, threw it back, with a contemptuous, 'Take it, drunkard!' and went on with his scolding of the Senate. If the occasion were less serious, he concluded, he would be only too pleased to see them suffer for their slackness. As it was, he gave his vote for the only proper punishment for high treason.

Cato had always the power of the single-minded in creating immediate effects. And, on this occasion, one rapid and irrevocable action was in question. The conspirators were condemned and executed within a few hours. Caesar took his defeat in silence. Cato, leading the Senate, hailed Cicero 'The Father of his Country' – a fact which Cicero never afterwards forgot, nor allowed anyone else to forget.

The danger was not over. Catiline was at large in Italy, raising armies of the unemployed. Murena, an experienced general, was chosen consul-elect, with a view to leading the campaign against him. But Murena, like everyone else, had used bribery to secure his election; and the facts came to Cato's knowledge. Before the year was out, Cato was accusing and Cicero defending, Murena in the law courts.

Cicero, like a ju-jitsu wrestler, used his opponent's strength against him. He made, in fact, a statement of the Man of the World's case against the Stoic. Cato's accusation, he admits, amounts almost to a pre-decision; but the true Roman way is to discount excessive strength in an accuser. Of course, Cato is right; he is always right. He is so right that he is wrong. His principles are 'more harsh and hard than either truth or nature allow.' He follows Zeno's maxims: – A wise man is never moved by influence; never pardons offences; no one is merciful except the fool and the waverer; it is unmanly to be won or appeased by entreaties. Philosophers alone are handsome, though they be deformed; rich, though in beggary; kings, though in slavery. The ruck of us are renegades, exiles, enemies, madmen. All sins are equally heinous; the philosopher never supposes anything; never hesitates; never mistakes; nor changes his mind. Cato holds these views not just for argument like most people, but as a rule of life. Let us hope that age and experience may mellow him and teach him some tolerance. Already, he is perhaps himself a little politer to people before than after an election. Murena has gone a little further – he has treated a few of them – what normal man has not? And Murena is urgently needed by his country. The consul who has saved the city pleads for the successor who can carry on his work.

Cicero, as usual, got his client off. And, though there is nothing to show that Murena had much to do with it, Catiline and his friends were finally disposed of in the next year.

Though the conditions were rather different, the Romans appear to have regarded law-court pleadings very much as they are regarded in modern society. The rough and tumble of legal attack and defence was a game to itself with its own rules and scores and reverses; and it was not assumed that grudges between the pleaders would persist. Cicero's telling attack, with so suave a neatness catching Stoicism and Cato at their weakest point, was special pleading; everyone knew that he was himself a philosopher, with much sympathy for Stoic principles. Nevertheless, such things are not easily forgotten. 'What a witty consul we have!' was Cato's only comment at the time. Perhaps his later treatment of Cicero would have been precisely the same – it was sufficiently in character – if the Murena case had never occurred. Such matters are trifles to the Stoic, not worth a second thought. But they also happen to be the things that human nature forgives least easily. The only two men who had a fighting chance against the Big Bosses can hardly have loved each other the better for it.

But the little bosses were alarmed. Caesar had been forced to try his strength too soon, and had taken a fall. It looked almost as if the uncomfortable old days, when men had to be what they seemed, and earn what they got, might be coming back. Caesar and his friends decided that they had rather, on the whole, have Pompey back than be left at the mercy of these impossible Stoics. There followed one of the violent and ridiculous scenes made inevitable by the checkmating veto system. Caesar was now a praetor, his ally, Metellus, a tribune. They decided to put the decree recalling Pompey to the popular assembly and, on voting day, filled the forum with armed slaves and gladiators.

But Cato, also, was a tribune. He walked unarmed through the midst of the gangsters and sat down between Caesar and Metellus, interrupting their conversation. A strange, undignified contest followed, Metellus trying to read the decree, Cato forbidding him to do so. In the riot that followed, Cato was extricated from a shower of sticks and stones literally under the mantle of the consul, Murena, whose accuser he had been. There was a day of tumult and intrigue, and yet once more, Cato carried his point, and Metellus, only saved from deposition by Cato's own intervention, went off in disgust to Asia to report to his master.

Pompey, however, was an easy-going person, though no gentleman – 'No good breeding, no straightforwardness, no political morality, no distinction, no courage, no liberality,' is Cicero's probably prejudiced comment. But he had the vulgar man's good-nature – he believed in 'living and letting live,' whenever it was possible. When he came home in the ordinary course in the next year, he decided that it would be less trouble to make a friend of Cato than to have him always snapping at his ankles. He must have hoped, in spite of rumour, that the uncompromising young man whose back he had been so glad to see a few years before, might by this time have acquired some sense of reality. He proposed that both himself and his son should marry into Cato's family.

The chronicles differ as to whether it was Cato's nieces or daughters who were the proposed brides. As Cato was at this time still in the early thirties, it seems unlikely that they could have been his daughters, though early marriages were usual. But the uncertainty in itself illustrates the assumed unimportance of domestic life in the career of a Roman of the governing classes. Plutarch, in his 'life,' gives about a page to Cato's domestic affairs, adding, with regard to the last episode that he describes, 'This was done at a later time, but, since I was speaking of women, I thought it well to mention it now.' Shakespeare is merely translating freely when he puts into Portia's mouth:

> *I grant I am a woman, but withal*
> *A woman whom Lord Brutus took to wife.*
> *I grant I am a woman, but withal,*
> *A woman well reputed, Cato's daughter.*
> *Think you I am no stronger than my sex,*
> *Being so fathered, and so husbanded?*

Women and wives being so incidental, we get very few glimpses of our righteous man's home life, though these few are illuminating. He was, says Plutarch, again as a matter of small importance, 'unfortunate in the female part of his family.' It may, indeed, have been relatively unimportant to Cato, for there are indications that the great love of his life had been disposed of while he was still a very young man, in the death of his brother, Caepio, over whom he had mourned more deeply and performed costlier funeral rites than was considered quite becoming in a Stoic. There are no other signs of any weakness of the affections in Cato's life, no apparent deviations from the Stoic maxim that one should do only those things for which one could give good reason to a disinterested person.

He had come a virgin to his first wife, Atilia, in accordance with Stoic principles, which held that sexual relations were justified only when children were wanted. Atilia's principles were apparently less rigid, for she was divorced for unfaithfulness after the birth of two children. Cato's sister, Servilia, the mother of Brutus, not only smirched the family record, but chose Caesar to do it with. Cato's second wife, Marcia, appears to have been of the more docile temperament suitable for the mate of a man who was always right.

But, if women and wives were in themselves unimportant, children and blood relationships were important. The women of Cato's family were delighted by Pompey's proposals. These would be great matches. One can imagine their sighs of helpless resignation when the answer went back that Cato was not accessible from the women's chamber. He was highly honoured by the offer, he added, but Pompey could expect his support in any case so long as his actions were just. In the meantime, he preferred not to give hostages against his country's safety.

Pompey turned elsewhere for his wife, and found her in Caesar's daughter.

It was, in fact, the doom of republican Rome as well as the turning-point in Cato's career. Cato did not know it and went on fighting stubbornly, sometimes making a small score, constantly suffering big defeats. For the Stoic, to whom all virtues, as all sins, are one and equal, perhaps the small scores were as important as the big ones would have been. All good actions, great and small, successful or not, go into the weaving of the completely righteous life. On public affairs, the effect of that righteous life was from this time almost negligible. Cato had renounced the rôle of the saviour of Rome for the salvation of his personal integrity.

It is the eternal problem of the well-intentioned politician. If one makes no concessions, one becomes isolated and helpless; if one begins to make them, there is no certain stopping-place. Once his integrity had been compromised by the alliance with Pompey, Cato might well have 'mellowed' into a typical Roman politician. He preferred to remain the waspish Stoic, reduced to the futile stabbing in and out of his sting.

The two super-spiders, Pompey and Caesar, now began weaving in concert. Pompey was lazy, and saw no reason why Caesar should not do the work for him. Caesar's latest idea was a scheme of mass bribery. He brought in laws for distributing land and grain to the Roman masses, and it was as hopeless to oppose them as it would be for a British Government now to try to withdraw the dole, or Old Age Pensions. The Senate was not only compelled to accept a law handing over the Campania to the people; but every individual senator was legally ordered to take an oath that he would maintain that law and never advocate its repeal.

Here was an issue of a kind hardly allowed for in the Stoic code. Cato believed that the people should be re-settled on the land – it was the obviously sensible solution of one of Rome's worst problems. But he knew the intention of this particular measure. He had spoken and voted against it. And a Stoic 'never hesitates; never blunders; never changes his mind.' But if he now refused to take the oath, he could be ruined and exiled, and who would then be left to carry on the fight?

Cicero dressed the situation up handsomely for him. Was it justifiable, after all, to disobey laws passed by duly constituted authority? And to disobey would destroy his future usefulness. 'Though Cato have no need of Rome, yet Rome has need of Cato, and so, too, have all his friends.' Cicero was wrong. Cato could be of no more use to Rome except as a spiritual monument. And yet, he made his concession, now that it was too late; and took the oath, last of all, except for his disciple, Favonius.

Caesar continued to set problems in casuistry without mercy. He intended to immobolise this large wasp, once for all, as well as that less formidable, but loudly buzzing, bluebottle, Cicero. Cicero had now quarrelled with Clodius, the new tribune. He had given evidence against him in Caesar's suit for a scandal caused in his house at the time of the Vestal Rites, when Clodius had got in disguised as a woman – the episode which resulted in the divorce of Caesar's wife on the famous 'above suspicion' principle. Caesar and Clodius, as practical politicians, were now friends again, and Cicero was the common enemy. But the 'Father of his Country' would be more easily attacked in the absence of the man who had first hailed him so. And, just at this point, an ideal opening occurred to remove and discredit the righteous man at one blow.

Someone had to go to Cyprus on an unsavoury mission — to dispossess King Ptolemy, a Roman vassal, who had done no particular harm, but had the misfortune to be very rich. Cato was offered the appointment and indignantly refused. A special decree was at once passed ordering him to accept it. The dilemma recurred. It is wrong to disobey the orders of lawfully constituted authority; it is also wrong to commit unjust actions. Cato, already weakened by concession, for once tried to make things easy for himself. He sent a messenger to Ptolemy urging him to make a voluntary surrender and promising to look after him if he did. Ptolemy preferred to pick up the dropped logic of the Stoic; and committed suicide.

A more uncomfortable position for the righteous man can hardly be imagined. It must have given Cato, the ideal Cato, who was so intimately also the real Cato, the worst moral wound he ever received. But there was no outward sign of distress. He went to Cyprus and compensated himself by performing his mission with the most scrupulous exactness, although he had been given insultingly inadequate help. Every article of Ptolemy's treasure was valued and sold with a care for State interests that scandalised Cato's colleagues, accustomed to regard the wealth of the provinces as the natural perquisite of Roman officials. 'You have sent me to do your dirty work,' he told the citizens of Rome in effect. 'At least, you shall see that no one else can do it so well'; and he added a dramatic 'and be damned to you!' when the time came to return. The citizens were for making an occasion of it. They were delighted to get the treasure and to be sure that they were getting it all. They turned out in their thousands. Consuls and praetors came in procession down the Tiber to meet the incoming ships and welcome their faithful envoy. Cato sailed past them up the river without landing and brought his cargo into dock. Returning futile and humiliated, the Senate yet decreed him a special praetorship. He threw the honour back in their faces.

Cato was thirty-seven when he was thus shelved, deliberately sent out of the way on a dishonouring mission, while Caesar and his friends did what mischief they liked. He could not miss the point so brutally rammed home. He must have begun to realise his failure as a statesman and to suspect that his rejection of Pompey's friendship had been virtually the end of his career. There remained the righteous life, scratched and muddied as it had been. One makes the most of the only thing one has. A certain theatrical gusto, a touch of caricature, beginning with the insulting gesture of the return, seems to creep into the righteous life about this point.

Another glimpse of Cato in his more intimate relationships appears in Plutarch's account of the Cyprus episode. Munatius, Cato's closest personal friend, coming to complain of his quarters, found him closeted with a new associate, Canidius, and was sent away. Not unnaturally, he displayed a little jealousy such as most men would have taken with a gently flattered amusement. For Cato, it was an occasion for a lecture on the folly of too much love and its tendency to rouse aversion in the object. No doubt, the Stoic would have held that all rational statements may fitly be made at all times by all rational men, and there was therefore no reason why the too-much-loved one should not himself say this to the over-enthusiastic lover, nor yet why the conversation should not be repeated to the object of his jealousy. Cato expressed a pained surprise when Munatius would not come the next time he was sent for. He used his official position, and threatened to confiscate Munatius' goods. But Munatius made his sacrifice to irrationality and sailed for Rome.

The difference between the two philosophers continued for some time with a queer childishness, and, like children, they had to be reconciled. Neither apologised. Marcia, Cato's wife, 'contrived to have them both invited to sup together at the house of one Barca; Cato came in last of all, when all the rest were laid down and asked where he should be. Barca answered him where he pleased; then, looking about, he said he would be near Munatius, and went and placed himself next to him; yet he showed him no other mark of kindness all the time they were at table together. But, another time, at the entreaty of Marcia, Cato wrote to Munatius that he desired to speak with him. Munatius went to his house in the morning, and was kept by Marcia till all the company was gone; then Cato came, threw both his arms about him, and embraced him very kindly and they were reconciled.'

Yet Marcia herself shortly afterwards became the object of an experiment in rationality. Cato's friend and disciple, Hortensius, was anxious to ally himself with Cato's family and asked for his daughter, Portia, although she was already married, on the grounds that a woman of such sound origin should bear as many children as possible in the prime of her youth, and, if one man could not afford to have them, then others should be allowed their chance. Cato would not agree for his daughter (possibly her husband objected) but, instead, gave Hortensius his own wife until she should have borne him a child; after which, he took her back again. Marcia's own views on the transaction are nowhere recorded. But even in the Rome of that day, with all standards in flux and women of so little account, the episode was regarded doubtfully. There is a sentence in Quintilian, given to illustrate a point in logic. 'What difference is there between the question whether it was an honourable act on the part of Cato to make over Marcia to Hortensius, or whether such an action is becoming to a virtuous man?' There was such difference of opinion about the matter that it had become a stock problem of the philosophers.

The theoretical grounds of Cato's action can easily be inferred by anyone who has read Plato's *Republic*. Obviously, as Hortensius had pointed out, it is rational that the best people should have as many children as possible without regard to such irrelevancies as personal predilections, egotism or jealousy. And yet there is a certain superfluous violence in such deliberate flouting of moral sentiment. This was no longer a question of maintaining integrity, but of militant eccentricity. Cato, in his youth, said Plutarch, had disliked eccentricity for its own sake; he became conspicuous merely because he would not go out of his way to conform. But, now the Cyprus episode had occurred; and perhaps some such assertion in the little domestic world that he could control was necessary to restore the lost balance of the ideal Cato.

For in the larger political world, unlooked-for bedevilments continued. Even the Cyprus gesture did not come off perfectly. Cato, indeed, disdainfully delivered the dead Ptolemy's treasure to the last farthing. It was later to replenish Caesar's resources when he entered Rome as a conqueror, but the Stoic had done his distasteful duty, and, even if the possibility of such an outcome had occurred to him, he would doubtless have said that it was none of his business. It was another unexpected twist of circumstances that threatened to make the righteous man's retort look futile.

Events had followed the expected course in his absence. The 'Father of his Country' had been exiled for his treatment of the Catiline conspirators as soon as Cato was safely away. Pompey, idling at his country villa, had kept carefully out of it. But presently, the irresponsible Clodius had done something to offend him also, and Cicero's friends seized the opportunity to bring him back. He had taken his exile with wailings, 'disheartened and disconsolate, like an unfortunate lover.' Now, restored to Rome and honour, he was filled with the rage of a child that has been unjustly punished. He used his legal skill to find a flaw in Clodius' qualifications for his tribuneship. If he were allowed to make out his case, it would follow that Clodius' term of office and everything that had been done in it, became invalid, and this would include, not only Cicero's exile, but Cato's appointment and all his actions in connection with the Cyprus treasure. Rome's title to its possession would again become uncertain; and the great gesture would be as if it had never been. The citizens of Rome were not concerned about Cato's gesture; but they did not want there to be any doubt about the money. Cato pointed out this difficulty. Clodius was bad enough, he added, and he would gladly support any indictment against him for his behaviour when in office; but it would be an unworthy quibble to say now that his election was invalid. The right thing must not be done on the wrong grounds. Cicero lost his case. And the friendship between the two just men 'became more reserved.'

Cato had now quarrelled with everyone of importance – Caesar, the real enemy, Pompey, who could probably have been managed by a firm and skilful hand, and Cicero, his natural ally. The Triumvirate had formed – Caesar, Pompey and Crassus – a moral nonentity, but the richest man in Rome. They did what they liked, filled all offices with their nominees, passed any law they pleased.

Caesar, the most vigorous, chose Gaul for his province, and started on his career as a conqueror. With him away, there was a lull in Rome; enslavement was mild, though real. He had left one of his friends and his father-in-law as consuls. 'The empire,' said Cato, with more irony than perhaps he realised, 'had become a mere matrimonial agency.'

Such remarks can be a great consolation. The righteous man, in the practical sphere, had been reduced to the stature of a street-urchin shouting insults and playing tricks. But he had the street-urchin's freedom and gusto. It is not, after all, bad sport to be the one righteous man among the corrupt. If one does not live in a glass house, one can throw stones with a light heart. Cato made the most of his opportunities.

Cicero describes the situation about this time. 'Meanwhile a genuine statesman is not to be found even "in a dream." The man who could be one, my friend, Pompey – for such he is, as I would have you know – defends his twopenny embroidered toga by saying nothing. Crassus never risks his popularity by a word. The others you know without my telling you. They are such fools that they seem to expect that, though the Republic is lost, their fishponds will be safe. There is one man who does take some trouble, but rather, as it seems to me, with consistency and honesty, than with either prudence or ability – Cato. He has been for the last three months worrying those unhappy *publicani* who were formerly devoted to him, and refuses to allow of an answer being given them by the Senate. And so we are forced to suspend all decrees on other subjects until the *publicani* have got their answer. For the same reason, I suppose even the business of the foreign embassies will be postponed.'

The righteous man continued to throw stones with

a happy and impartial abandon. He was wounded in a riot when Domitius, the only man who had dared to stand for the consulship against Pompey and Crassus, was driven by force from the polling-station. Then he himself stood for the praetorship. Pompey and Crassus promptly passed a law providing that the praetors should enter their office immediately on election, so rendering them immune from accusations for bribery. Even so, Cato was expected to win, but a corrupted augur declared a bad omen, so that the election was postponed until enough of the voters had been bought.

He raised another riot by obstructive tactics, over a law which allowed consuls to raise armies in the provinces; but the law was passed. Over the next law, which still further increased Caesar's powers, he actually went to Pompey and pointed out that he was taking an Old Man of the Sea upon his shoulders; but that law passed also.

At last he obtained his praetorship, and proceeded to shock the public by going into court shoeless and in an old tunic. His vigorous campaign against corruption culminated in an attack on him by an angry mob.

Cato's personal prestige was still enormous, and his voice was powerful. He talked to the mob, and it went away. The cowering Senate sent congratulations. 'But I,' Cato told them, 'cannot congratulate you, who abandoned your praetor in danger.' He then invented an ingenious insurance against bribery. Candidates for office had to deposit large sums with him, which would be forfeited if he found them out in corrupt practices. Pompey retaliated by putting up Clodius to accuse him of having embezzled some of the Cyprus money – a farcical accusation, which merely caused delay and trouble, and was possible only because the accounts had been lost at sea.

So the righteous man tried to drive back the waves with

a broom, while Caesar swept like a hurricane through Gaul and on to Germany and Britain, becoming a religion to his soldiers.

In Rome, holding the yearly games, Cato awarded crowns of wild olive instead of golden ones. The people were more amused than annoyed – the crowns would not go to them – and flocked to his sports in preference to his rival's. On another occasion, he was present at the games of Flora, a carnival affair. At a given moment, when the people called for it, the female comedians would throw off their garments. But, for this time, the dénouement hung fire. A bashful uneasiness seemed to have descended upon the crowd. After a few moments, Favonius whispered to his grave-eyed friend and rounds of applause rang out as Cato left the field.

'Why, Cato severe, did you come into the theatre?' runs Martial's epigram on the incident, 'and, having come, why did you go?'

In such fields, the righteous man could still make his effect; and that equivocal applause of the relieved citizens was mankind's doubtful tribute to something less immediate (but can anyone certainly say less vital?) than the feats that brought the passionate 'Imperator!' from the throats of Caesar's soldiers.

In Caesar's absence, and Pompey's slackness, politics in Rome quickly became impossible. Elections were no longer carried merely by bribery. They were becoming like the Chicago elections of our own day. Armed gangsters occupied the polling stations and clashed freely in the forum and the streets; no one's life was safe. Pompey was the only man who could restore order, and it presently became clear that Pompey would have to be not merely allowed, but entreated, to do so. It was another dilemma for the Stoic. At last, he supported a motion to make

Pompey sole consul, with the grudging concession, 'Any government is better than none.'

So Pompey and Cato were more or less friends again at last. They met and embraced; and the whitewashed boss politely asked for the righteous man's advice and assistance in his difficult responsibility. The righteous man welcomed the convert. He had had no more animus against Pompey in the past, he said, than he now had affection for him. He should certainly have his advice in private, if he asked for it; and he should have it in public whether he wanted it or not.

Pompey, undiscouraged, continued to be pleased with himself in his new rôle. He had always wanted to be on good terms with everyone, and to have things running smoothly. People had sometimes misunderstood him, but that was all over now. He would clear up for them with pleasure this mess into which they had contrived to get themselves, and everyone should see how truly well-intentioned he was. He was so thorough about it, that Cato himself had to protest against his drastic laws being made retrospective – a measure which would have put half Rome in the dock. But, naturally, the man who had done all this for his fellow-citizens, expected a little latitude for himself and his friends. Cato was soon stopping his ears in the Courts against Pompey's illegal special pleading for a protégé.

Cato was now over forty and eligible for the highest office in Rome – the consulship. The prospect seemed to have improved. Pompey, at least on the surface, had reformed everyone but himself. The consulship was still a key position. Perhaps the righteous man was, after all, to have his chance. His opponents could not now openly buy the voters. But Cato wished to make sure. Canvassing by bodies of partisans was still allowed and it was impossible to keep watch on everything that went on. Before he stood for the consulship, he put a decree through the Senate providing that only the candidates themselves should be allowed to solicit votes.

The measure was decisive in the opposite direction to that intended. The electors were now free to vote according to their own unbiased opinion. And their opinions did not favour the man who had not only been the chief agent in diverting useful cash from their pockets, but was now taking away the bloom from their one moment of importance. No longer would they be flattered and cajoled by their betters; no longer could they snub the gilded youths who despised them for the rest of the year. And Cato's own idea of soliciting votes seemed to them a poor substitute. He lost the election.

Cato refused to be humiliated, omitting the odd customary 'mourning' of the defeated candidate. It had been a fair contest, he said. Evidently the people disliked his manners. But no honest man altered his manners to suit other people. He would never stand for any office again. And he kept his word.

But, if he could not help, he could still hinder – even his friends when they showed themselves more human than rational. Cicero was now governor of Cilicia. He had done well there; he had staved off a war by diplomacy, purified the administration, and broken up a dangerous horde of bandits, for which he had been hailed 'Imperator' by his army. But his vanity was still suffering from that undeserved exile, and he longed for the spectacular vindication of a Roman Triumph. No one could have more influence in such a case than Cato, for the senate, not the people, decreed the *Supplicatio* that must come first. It was difficult to ask Cato for a favour, but the longing would not be denied.

It was so important that the request should be perfectly put that discomfort and apology shout from every line of it. It begins with a brief, business-like account of Cicero's military and political achievements and goes on 'I shall consider that the highest possible compliment has been paid me, if you give me your vote in favour of a mark of honour being bestowed upon me.' Of course it is quite usual, he hastens to add, for men of the most respectable character to ask and grant such favours, 'yet I think in your case it is rather a reminder which is called for from me.' Cato has praised him so often, and his praise has been more valued than any other man's. Cato voted to give him a *Supplicatio* on that great occasion when he saved the State. They have always been comrades facing common enemies and dangers. He, too, has praised Cato, 'which I do not regard as constituting any claim on your gratitude, but as a frank expression of genuine opinion.'

Of course, Cato will want to know why he should attach so much value to such a trifle. He will answer frankly. No one could be more averse than himself to empty and vulgar praise. His exile was no disgrace; but he would like something to cancel it. He asks for this as a vindication on condition that Cato thinks his services deserve it – as surely, he must. Cato always considers character, too, in giving and withholding favours; and Cicero's administration has been equitable and pure. He has restored the loyalty of the allies; the provinces will speak for him.

Finally, he calls in philosophy as a last resort and alludes to their sympathies in tastes and studies. They two are the only practising philosophers.

It is a long and eloquent letter. And its length and eloquence serve only to bring out the fact that the defeat of a horde of bandits was not the kind of victory for which a Roman Triumph was the appropriate reward. Cicero was a better pleader for other men than for himself.

Cato wrote some time later to explain why he had not voted for Cicero's *Supplicatio*, which had, however, been granted without his help.

'I am glad to do as the public interest and our friendship alike prompt me, in expressing my joy that you are applying the same courage, integrity, and energy in your military command abroad as you displayed in time of crisis at home when a civilian, and therefore what I could conscientiously do, I did; that is, I commended by speech and vote your achievements in defending the province by your rectitude and good judgment, in saving King Areobazanes and his kingdom, and winning back the allies to loyalty.

'As to the *Supplicatio*, if you really prefer that we should thank the gods rather than yourself for a success that was in no way a matter of chance, but due to your own ability and self-restraint, then I am glad that it has been decreed. But, if you think a *Supplicatio* is a certain prelude to a Triumph, and for that reason wish good luck to have the credit rather than yourself, remember that a Triumph does not always follow a *Supplicatio*, and that it is a much finer thing than any Triumph to have the Senate's judgment that your own good management and honourable dealing have saved the province rather than armed force or divine favour; and that was what I meant by my vote.

'And I have written to you at greater length than I usually write, because I am most anxious for you to believe that I tried to get for you what I thought would be for your highest honour, and that I am glad that you have what you wanted more.

'Farewell, and keep your regard for me and manage your journey so as to ensure your good services for the Republic and the allies in the future.'

Probably, Cato regarded this as a particularly tactful letter, even if there lingered at the back of his mind, with the grim irony which is the righteous man's legitimate diversion, Cicero's own mocking words at the Murena trial. 'The wise man is never moved by influence . . . it is unmanly to be won or appeased by entreaties . . . Cato holds these views not just for argument like most people, but as a rule of life. . . . Let us hope that time may mellow him and teach him some tolerance.'

Cicero's reply is outwardly good-tempered. It could hardly be otherwise He had asked for it. He begs Cato 'still to be glad if I have the good fortune to get what I myself have preferred.' To other correspondents, he was less careful. The incident, he complains, has been difficult to explain away to his friends. And, to Atticus, he confides that Cato 'has been disgracefully spiteful.' He has actually voted for a *Supplicatio* for someone else.

So the philosopher alienated his friends for incontestably good reasons, while the practical man was rapidly reaching the point when he needed no friends, or, at least, no equal ones. A bigger man than Cicero was demanding his *Supplicatio* and his Triumph. Caesar had attacked the Germans when they believed a truce to be still in force and routed them with a loss of three hundred thousand. The philosophic street urchin got in a last delightful impertinence. He proposed that Caesar should be surrendered to the Germans as a truce-breaker. And he analysed Caesar's career in the Senate House in such a manner that even the fishpond experts were alarmed and began to dally with the idea of recalling Caesar and appointing his successor. It was all that was necessary.

Caesar replied that he would disband his army and resign his provinces if Pompey would do the same. The consul, Marcellus, chose the moment to flog one of Caesar's pet Gallic 'citizens,' so denying their citizenship in the most drastic and insulting manner. Then things began to happen quickly. With hardly a perceptible pause, Caesar had crossed the Rubicon and was marching on Rome.

Pompey, hastily appointed Dictator, had not his resources ready. His influence and the armies that would follow him, were in the East. The constitutional party was forced to abandon Rome.

Cato, not omitting his 'I told you so's,' went with them, and no one had leisure to point out that his had been the type of prophecy that precipitates its own fulfilment. He went with little heart. To fight for either Caesar or Pompey was not the kind of choice that should be presented to a Stoic. And, as usual, he took his revenge by gesture. Henceforth, until the end, he went into mourning for his country, allowed his hair and beard to grow, and refused to recline at meals after the Roman custom.

For the moment, he did little else. Sicily was left in his charge by Pompey, and was soon threatened by overwhelming forces. A strong stand there could not have succeeded, but might have gained valuable time. But humanity (kept duly under control) is a first duty with a Stoic. Cato would not – for Pompey's sake – have a devastated country on his conscience. He abandoned Sicily and followed Pompey to Greece, where all his advice was now in the direction of delay and temporising. Accordingly, he lost the command of the navy which Pompey had been about to give him. If everything, after all, went well, it might later be inconvenient to have so lukewarm a supporter at the head of a powerful force.

The slight had no apparent effect on Cato's sentiments. Having inspired the soldiers by a stirring speech before the battle of Dyracchium, he chilled their victory by mourning over their fallen fellow-countrymen afterwards. Pompey kept him away from the battle of Pharsalia, where Caesar struck his decisive blow.

Pompey fled to Egypt and his followers scattered. And the Stoic was left, in his element, at last, fighting a rear-guard action against desperate odds, but with the issues clear. He was out of the Hell of doubt and hesitation, and the physical Hell of defeat and hardship appeared a pleasant change. Holding his small detachment together, he joined Pompey's son, who had the fleet, at Corcyra. There they found Cicero on the point of ratting back to Italy. Cato saved his life from young Pompey's fury, and let him go. It was the last meeting of the two righteous men and practising philosophers, as no doubt they both guessed; but there is no record of their conversation. Cato then sailed after Pompey towards Egypt, but was turned back by the news of his betrayal and murder. Lucan perhaps uses his poetic licence in suggesting that Cato rejoiced at the news, but it certainly cleared the stage still further. It remained now only to play out the righteous life to the end. There is almost an artistic frenzy of creation in Cato's conduct of his last year of life.

He took his little force to Cyrene, and there heard that other allies of Pompey, Scipio and King Juba, were consolidating themselves away to the West in Numidia. There followed a march that almost attained the legendary fame of the march of the Ten Thousand, or the great marches of the Conquistadors through South American jungles. As in most legends, details have been confused. Plutarch gives it as a seven days' march; Strabo as thirty, Lucan as two months. However that may be, Cato brought his men across the desert, through the dangers of thirst, famine and hostile savages. He marched on foot with them the whole way. When they came to a spring, he was the last to drink; except when it was suspected of having been poisoned, when he was the first. Many men died of snakebite in a variety of agonies minutely described by Lucan, in spite of the help of a native tribe who were said to be immune to snake poison. But the soldiers' complaints died away whenever Cato approached. When at last they reached signs of cultivation again, they welcomed them as the Greeks had hailed the sea in Pontus.

It was a perfect interlude. But in Numidia, even now, politics were waiting again. King Juba, an independent and quite unreliable ally, and Scipio, the Roman governor, were holding the province. The army called upon Cato to take the supreme command and Scipio offered to stand aside. But Scipio was a pro-consul and Cato had never been more than a praetor. The people had not liked his manners enough. It was against the law for the subordinate to command the man of higher official rank; and Cato was only in the fight at all to defend the laws. He insisted that Scipio, a headstrong and incompetent person, should keep the command. And Scipio, since he had it, insisted on having it completely. Caesar, as usual, had done the unexpected; discourteously ignoring the convention against winter campaigns, he was in Numidia before anyone had thought it possible. Cato had meanwhile won over the city of Utica by his fair dealing; and the citizens had helped him to fortify it. He proposed to use it as a base, and carry on the guerilla campaign against Caesar which the country and the conditions seemed to make most promising. Scipio told him that he was a coward, threw his whole army at

Caesar's at Thapsus, and received a defeat from which no recovery was possible. Cato himself in Utica was the only force left to oppose Caesar in Africa.

It was now a question of a few days at best. But Cato addressed the Romans in Utica and almost persuaded them to hold out. Rome had recovered from more desperate situations, he said, and, in any event, nothing worse than a glorious death could happen to them. There was a burst of enthusiasm. They would hand over all their property, free their slaves, and fight to the last man. But Cato did not like enthusiasm. It was only fair, he told them, that they should deliberate before they committed themselves. He himself would go away while they talked it over. The deliberation had the result that might be expected; a glorious death lost its attraction with Cato no longer present. The decision to fight was abandoned, and the city lapsed into confusion. Cato sent word to his fugitive allies not to come there, but by sheer moral bullying brought in a stray troop of Roman horse to cover the escape of the citizens. It was still possible to get away by sea, and he was determined that those who were likely to be made scapegoats should do so. The rest must make their peace with Caesar. All the gates were shut except that which gave on to the harbour; and Cato set himself to organise the evacuation, and the food supplies of those that were left. His disregard of self had become conspicuous. As Plutarch naïvely puts it, 'it was easily perceived that he had determined to die, though he tried not to let it appear.'

Many of Cato's personal friends were packed off with the rest. A young man who wished to stay and share his fate was forbidden to do so. Lucius Caesar, a kinsman of the conqueror, offered to try to make Cato's peace for him. He would, he said, feel it an honour to kneel to Caesar for that purpose. He was answered that Caesar had no right either to kill or to save Cato. The young man who had wished to stay had not gone, and declared that he would do whatever Cato did. Cato surrendered the point with a smiling, 'We shall see.'

On the evening of this busy day, Cato held a banquet with his remaining friends, followed by the usual entertainment, a philosophic discussion. They debated the Stoic principle 'that the good man only is free, and that all the wicked are slaves.' Cato fell so hotly upon the Peripatetic philosopher who opposed him, that there was a sudden silence; and then an abrupt outbreak of conversation about the practical business of the evacuation.

Suicide had an important place in the Stoics' code. When circumstances became intractable, the good man was at liberty, if not obliged, to make a dignified exit from a world which was no fit place for him. The modern view of suicide as cowardly seems never to have occurred to the ancients; and, indeed, one may well have a misgiving whether that idea may not sometimes have served as cover for a more poignant bodily cowardice. To the Stoic, if there was sufficiently good reason for it, 'so that one could convince another person of it without rhetoric,' a man might and should kill himself as simply as he would do any other action for which there was good reason. 'Remember,' said Epictetus, 'that the door is open; be not more cowardly than children; but, as they say when the thing does not please them, "I will play no longer," so do you say in like case, "I will no longer play," and be gone; but, if you stay, do not complain.'

Life in the Roman world no longer pleased Cato. It had become incompatible with his own game. Already he had been many times manœuvred into equivocal positions. 'Keep clear of politics,' he had lately warned his son, 'there is no room for Catos there.' If he now surrendered to Caesar, he would probably be kept alive on Caesar's well-known principle of preferring living trophies to dead ones. And life at Caesar's mercy would be, for Cato, a series of paradoxes. The work of art – the 'good life' – to which he had devoted himself would be hopelessly defaced. Now, it was still in his power to give it the final touch of perfection.

It was, in fact, necessary for the good man to die. Otherwise it might so well all have been a pose. And a pose of course in one sense, the modern sense, it had been – what the Americans call a 'personality picture,' since ideals are the most artificial of all that is made by art. But the matter is not so simple as all that. One might make out a case for defining man as the 'animal that poses,' and one would merely have said, in other words, that man is the animal that thinks, the animal that imagines, the animal that creates – almost working round to the Stoic definition of man as 'the rational animal.' But, to make that good, the pose must be carried through.

One could not be the rudest man in Rome, throw stones freely, play the *enfant terrible* in the senate-house and not be prepared to die rather than submit to Caesar.

Yet the book that Cato took into his room after his guests had dispersed in dismayed silence, was not the maxims of his master, Zeno, nor any work of the Stoic philosophers; but the *Phaedo*, the dialogue in which Socrates gives his proof of the immortality of the soul. Stoic doctrine on the future life was doubtful; perhaps the good man survived death, perhaps he survived for a time, perhaps not at all. It did not matter, the good life was sufficient in itself. Yet the choice of the *Phaedo* suggests that it cannot have been quite easy for so vigorous a vitality to deny itself. It was perhaps well for Cato's resolution that he had provided himself with an expectant audience.

The audience did not help practically, if it did so morally. There is something peculiarly shocking about death deliberately planned and contemplated. Cato's friends clearly understood his necessity, and yet they could not endure to be parties to his solution. Looking up from his reading, he saw that his sword had been removed. It must have relieved pressure to storm at the servants and scold his weeping son. He even injured his hand in striking one of them. They had, of course, to give in. A little boy brought the sword back.

Cato read the *Phaedo* twice, and apparently slept half the night, for he was heard snoring. Then he enquired after the fugitives and had his hand dressed. When news was brought that all were safely gone and the town quiet, he sent away the messenger and immediately afterwards stabbed himself. His injured hand crippled him and the blow was not immediately effectual. There was a scene of horror in which the surgeon tried to bind him up and Cato tore the wound open again. Thus the righteous man's death was attained.

Destiny saw to it, wrote Seneca, that Cato should come to no harm, parodying the sonorous Latin of the charge to the consuls in time of danger to see that the State came to no harm. To modern scepticism, it seems rather that Cato had seen to it himself – made certain that, at least, the legendary figure which Cato had created should take no harm. He succeeded. Following generations of Romans, comfortable or discontented under the Emperors, made almost a god of him. All western languages have an adjective corresponding to our 'Catonian.' To have originated an adjective that has lasted two thousand years is perhaps as great an achievement in its way as conquering an enemy, or saving one's country.

But our sympathy will be rather with Cicero, who wrote, 'It may be said, Cato died a noble death. Well, that, at any rate, is in our power when we will. Let us only do our best to prevent its being necessary to us as it was to him.' So Cicero lived on another difficult and harried three years, and was at last chased and butchered in his litter by Antony's gangsters.

ACKNOWLEDGMENTS

THE writer is indebted to various authors and publishers for permission to use the following quotations from copyright sources: quotations from the translations of Cicero's *De Finibus* on page 5, lines 24–27, and on page 5, last line to line 2 on page 6; from *Tusculan Disputations*, lines 2–5 on page 6; from Quintilian's *Institutio Oratoria*, on pages 25 and 26, are from the Loeb Classical Library, published by Heinemann.

Quotations from translations of *Cicero's Letters* in Bohn's Library, published by G. Bell & Sons, are on pages 10, 19, 28, 33, 35, lines 15–16, and 43.

In Section I the quotations from Plutarch on pages 1, 11, 19, 20, 27, 28 are from the Dryden translation. Other translations in this Section not already mentioned are original.

II
THE CHRISTIAN

To the man of religious temperament, that is to say, the man who is impelled to establish some stable mental relationship with the universe in general, two attitudes are possible – that of the Stoic defiance and that of acceptance. He may feel that things in general are hostile, or that they are friendly. Not that even the defiant religious man can conceive himself as standing quite alone. He is driven to postulate some higher authority such as the Stoic's 'Law of Nature,' which, to us, seems so unnatural, or the Puritans' God. Nevertheless, his attitude to the world is Satanic; he is 'a pilgrim and a stranger, dwelling in the midst of foes.' He is not only not at home in the world, but has no desire to be so. He will carve his own way through the recalcitrant material at any cost whatever.

But there are also select souls born with a passion of friendliness for everything. They cannot believe in malignity. Occasionally, such fortunate temperaments may be so helped by circumstances that they go through life without vital disillusionment. They are charmed and charming. Everything and everyone conspires to give them a good time. They are born into a favourable environment and nothing happens to take them out of it. These are the sunny-tempered sportsmen, the delightful feminine women, whose mere presence is like a spring day. Such, perhaps, was the rich young man whom Jesus loved at sight, and whom He sent away sorrowful.

A rich young man of such temperament lived in the

Assisi of the thirteenth century. It was a pleasant time and place in which to be alive. Country and climate were enchanting. Assisi itself was small – we should probably call it a large village – but was, none the less, the centre of its little world, in the tide of the pageantry and drama of mediaeval life and of such culture as existed at the time. Francis Bernardone belonged to a privileged class – that of the wealthy merchants who were beginning to be an honoured minor aristocracy in the cities of Northern Italy. He was the family hero and was spoilt by admiring parents. He grew up a dandy and a poet. Though slight, he was active and athletic and had his share of physical courage; he could take a creditable part in the little city wars which seem to have been hardly more perilous for upper-class youths than a Rugby football-match, and were played with far more elegance and romantic display, according to the rules of chivalry. Between times, Francis helped his father in a desultory manner with his trade in fine cloths, but little else was expected of him except to exist gracefully and do his family credit among the gay young people of the town.

Francis, says one chronicler, 'was a merrier man than was his father, and more generous, given unto jests and songs, going round the city of Assisi day and night in company with his like, most freehanded in spending . . . beyond measure sumptuous in his clothes, using stuffs more costly than it beseemed him to wear . . . as though by nature courteous in manner and word after the purpose of his heart, never speaking a harmful or shameful word unto any. . . . Nay, indeed, though he were so gay and wanton a youth, yet of set purpose would he make no reply unto them that said shameful things unto him.' His parents grumbled sometimes when he would rush away in the middle of a meal to join some comrades who were calling for him, as parents are apt to grumble at the absences and outside enthusiasms of a popular child. But they were immensely proud of him. 'He is more like a prince than a son of ours,' his mother confided to the neighbours.

But this spoilt child was also sensitive. He not only liked everybody, but everybody must like him and be happy in his presence. The smallest discordance in his surroundings was to him like the pea under the seven mattresses to the true princess. Once, when he was bargaining with a customer in the market-place, a beggar began to pester him for alms. Absorbed in his business, Francis put him off sharply. When he had finished and looked round, the beggar had vanished. Francis dashed after him, searched the market and the streets and, finding him in a back alley, loaded him with money. On another occasion when he and a few comrades were prisoners in Perugia waiting for ransom, one of the little wars having gone against them, Francis's high spirits kept his comrades entertained. Their appreciation went to his head. 'You will see,' he announced expansively, 'one day I shall be adored by the whole world.' But one of the prisoners was for some reason cold-shouldered by the others – perhaps he had given away a goal, or its equivalent. This situation was unbearable to Francis, and he gave neither the outcast nor his boycotters any peace until he had drawn him back into the circle.

But it is not, after all, an easy world in which to like everything. There are, for instance, poverty, pain, disease, death and, more pervading than all, the perversity of other people. A life has to be carefully sheltered indeed, if it is never to come into vital contact with any of these things. An Indian king had once tried to perpetuate this Eden-like charm of existence for his young son. He kept him always in three palaces – one for the summer, one for the winter, and one for the rainy season – with lotus pools of blue, white and red lotus flowers in the gardens. The prince was clothed in robes of Benares cloth; day and night, a white umbrella was held over him to protect him from cold, heat, dust, chaff or dew; and in the rainy season, beautiful female musicians played for him. But, one day, the young man called his charioteer, and rode out and saw an unfamiliar figure in the road. It was bent, with white hair, leaning on a staff, and tottering as it walked. 'What has he done that his hair is not like that of other men, nor his body?' asked the young man of his charioteer. The charioteer replied that he was like that because he was old and had not much longer to live. 'Am I, too, subject to old age, then?' asked the prince, 'or am I out of reach of it?' The charioteer answered truthfully and the prince turned back home and became thoughtful.

He continued to be unfortunate in his rides. The next time he saw a sick man 'fallen and weltering,' while his friends tried to lift him and dress his sores. And, after that, a funeral. Last of all, he met a man in a yellow robe with a shaven head and was told that he was 'one who had gone forth.' The next day, young Gautama, too, had put on the yellow robe, and 'gone forth.'

The call of a magnificent adventure came to Assisi when Francis Bernardone was twenty-two. Gaulthier de Brienne was going, with the Pope's blessing, to claim the crown of Sicily, and was calling for recruits. This was something on a grander scale than the little inter-state wars. The youth of Assisi responded enthusiastically and, foremost among them, of course, Francis. Now, at last, he had his opportunity to make good his dreams of glory and honour. He bought himself a splendid equipment, and, then, meeting a poor knight in shabby kit, gave it all away to him. But, fine or shabby, he was determined to go, and the town resounded with all that he meant to do and all that he would become.

The expedition started; Francis went with it one day's march, and then was left behind. For some reason, the great adventure went on without him. There are a variety of explanations to choose from. He had just recovered from a bout of fever and probably, as is natural to sanguine temperaments, had insisted on recovering too soon and had a relapse. The Catholic story, on the other hand, is that he was turned back by a dream. Sabatier suggests, more plausibly, that his naïve boasting had roused his companions, among whom must have been strangers and hard-bitten old soldiers, to a more brutal teasing than the spoilt child could endure.

What is certain is that Francis came back to Assisi, victim of a humiliating anti-climax; and was obliged to stay there, a lonely Cinderella, while the comrades among whom he had been king, marched off to Sicily and its glorious opportunities. Such youthful tragedies have a poignancy that is often forgotten in maturer years. The one certain lesson of experience – that everything passes – has not yet been learnt. And Francis was unaccustomed to disappointment. Whether the disaster was the result of his own folly or merely misfortune, it must have seemed to him that life had suddenly, without reason, betrayed him. Most of his friends had gone, and those who were left were, no doubt, inclined to laugh at him. It was a situation such as almost inevitably produces a change of habit in an impressionable youth. Francis was driven into thought. He took to solitary walks and broodings in the woods and hills.

One day, when he was riding out of the city alone, he

came face to face with a revolting figure. Lepers had always had a peculiar horror for Francis – they were numerous and unescapable in those days – disgusting travesties of humanity, their state and sufferings beyond remedy. When he caught sight of one, he had been in the habit of hastily giving money to a servant to give him, while he stopped his nose and turned his back. But, this time, there was no servant at hand. Francis pulled up his horse, turned it; and then stopped short. Then he wheeled round again, dismounted, ran to the repulsive creature, embraced him and gave him all the money he had.

According to Catholic legend, when he looked back, there was no one to be seen. But the symbolic character of the incident needs no such miraculous enhancement.

Certainly, the young Francis of the care-free days must often have seen unpleasant objects and encountered the hard things of life. His habit with lepers shows his way with them. A healthy organism has a great capacity for ignoring what would be likely to disturb its balance if attended to. It is a painful, but very necessary, trait of human nature. For most of us, if our sympathetic instincts, which are yet vital to social existence, were quite unchecked, life would be hardly livable. Therefore, we develop a sense of humour about the minor misfortunes of our neighbours – and, sometimes, indeed, about the greater ones. Or, if that will not do, we take refuge, like the youthful Francis, in a sheer refusal to contemplate them. Whether such a refusal is, in fact, always a true escape is another question. Suppressed sympathy, like other suppressed instincts, has a way of breaking out in ugly sadistic forms.

Now, in this phase of lowered resistance brought on by his own wounded vanity, the things that the gay young Francis had successfully ignored kept cropping up. This, too, is a common experience – something strikes one's mind forcibly for the first time and, for a while afterwards, it seems to appear everywhere, in every conversation one hears, in every book or paper one picks up, so that some speculative minds have even been impelled to imagine a law of coincidence. Moreover, old memories return and take on a new significance in relation to the new impression. It was hardly necessary just then for Francis to meet actual lepers in the road. His imagination could supply them. 'The devil,' says Thomas of Celano, writing about those days, 'made him think of a certain woman, an inhabitant of his city, who was monstrously hunchbacked and presented a hideous sight to all; and he threatened to make him resemble her if he did not give up what he had begun.'

Those to whom pity has become a detached instinct, will shrug their shoulders at the young man whose reaction to misery was the fear that it might infect himself. But Francis's instinct of sympathy had not become detached. It was intimately connected with his vanity – for vanity is, after all, one phase of an intense consciousness of oneself in relation to other people. The dangerous precipice on the verge of which he was hovering was that of self-identification with everything, even with lepers and hunchbacks.

Probably most young people of intelligence and imagination who have emerged from a sheltered childhood, pass through some such ordeal, when something happens to bring home to them the reality of malign forces in the world. But, for most, the readjustment is gentler and more gradual. They have not all been spoilt children, and most of them have not the religious temperament that insists on moral harmony at all costs. They can find distractions; they can divide their minds into water-tight compartments. A smooth surface is soon formed over the irritating intruder and life goes on as before. One sympathises sometimes, when it is convenient and so far as it is convenient, and learns to shrug at the rest. No such easy compromise was possible to the young Francis. He must have a solution complete and absolute.

Francis is generally admitted to have been the typical Christian. It is a favourite exercise with the pious to draw the parallel between his life and that of Jesus Christ. But, in this earlier phase, the analogy with the Buddha, the young man who also met disconcerting figures in the road, seems far more striking. If Christianity had not existed in Francis's time and place, it is still inconceivable that he should have led a completely normal life. A defiant enemy of all the world he could never have been, but the third solution, the Buddha's solution, that of the withdrawal, might perhaps have been possible to him. To get rid of evil and suffering by the abnegation of all passion, even at last of compassion itself – there are signs that this alternative route had strong attractions for Francis. At several stages in his career he wavered towards the hermit life. And yet so foreign was isolation to his temper, that at the moment of his strongest impulse in this direction, he consulted Clare and Silvester whether he should yield to it. His friends gave the natural reply, and, in the enthusiasm of the reaction, Francis is said to have preached to the first congregation he could find, which happened to be a flock of birds.

If one cannot alter the world, nor yet retreat from it, and still must have it harmonious, the only course left is to alter oneself. And so during those two unhappy, morbid years, Francis effected the Christian transvaluation. Ugliness and suffering were there, no longer to be ignored. But everything must be lovable. Therefore ugliness and suffering were lovable. There was no escape from this logic. Things could not be what they seemed; for, if they were, an inadmissible conclusion resulted – that the universe was unfriendly. Therefore, the first must be the last, and the last, first; the meek must inherit the earth; one must 'love those who strike him upon the cheek.' The ideal man was the crucified convict. The passage already quoted from Thomas of Celano about the old hunchbacked woman continues: 'But the Lord of salvation and of grace encouraged him and he rejoiced as he heard this answer: "Francis," said God to him in the spirit, "thou shalt exchange what thou hast loved carnally and vainly for spiritual things; and, if thou wilt acknowledge Me, take thou the bitter instead of the sweet, and despise thyself, for the savour of the things whereof I speak shall be to thee reversed." ' To go back on one's senses, to find the odour of lepers agreeable, and the refuse of other men's meals pleasant to the palate, to feel insults and blows as a compliment and a kindness, one must have, in fact, a supernatural sanction. The passion of Jesus became to Francis the crux of his personal solution. Grief over the crucifixion was to become an obsession to him in later years, so that 'often when he rose from prayer, his eyes seemed full of blood.' And, blended with it, was, of course, the mystic exultation of one who has accepted 'the bitter for the sweet.' From his supreme moment of mystical emotion, Francis returned with the stigmata.

In this way, young Francis Bernardone decided what all thoughtful people at times try to decide – usually, to push the problem on one side again with a half-laughing, half-despairing *'solvitur ambulando'* – how he was to take the world. It remained to try the solution out – to see how the world was going to take him.

Francis had tremendous vitality and his impact on his surroundings, now that he was whole-souled again, could be no light matter. He had already begun to do odd and noticeable things. After the encounter on the road he had taken to visiting the pitiful warrens of the lepers in the rocks, carrying money and comforts. More strange still, he was polite to them, and presented his gifts as a matter of course between friends and equals. On a pilgrimage to Rome, he had changed garments and occupations for a day with a beggar outside St. Peter's. His words were often stranger even than his actions. The imagination of the dramatic poet began to work on the new material. At the last dinner he gave to his old companions, they made the usual joke about his absent-mindedness and were told that he had indeed found a beautiful new mistress. It was the creation of that fascinating personality, the princess of the new troubadours, 'Jongleurs de Dieu' – the 'Lady Poverty.'

How Francis's family, which had been so proud of his popularity and gay life, took the two years of solitary brooding and increasingly eccentric behaviour, is nowhere recorded. Probably, like most young people engaged in mental struggle, he concealed his state as far as possible, made plausible explanations or turned sulky when challenged. He was, at least, still living at home, an idle young man, now without even the justification of having a good time and showing up well among his contemporaries. No doubt, he still helped his father with his business sometimes, for the sequel shows that he was familiar with its details. It was a situation that inevitably led up to an explosion. The crisis when it came was the result of another intense emotional experience. He was praying before the crucified Christ in the ruined church of St. Damian when the figure seemed to him to move its lips and say, 'Restore my house.' The words came to him in their literal sense, though that does not, to a poet, to whom the symbol is of the essence of the thing, rule out also the symbolic overtones. But, for the moment, he saw only that his beloved master was unworthily housed in a ruin, and, having still the mental habits of the young aristocrat, immediately thought of setting builders to work. He had no money – perhaps his father was trying the effect of keeping him short, or perhaps he had given it all away. But he knew where there were bales of cloth belonging to the business. The need of the crucified Jesus obliterated every other consideration. He hurried home, made a parcel of the stuffs, mounted his horse and rode off to the Foligno market. There he made a quick sale of both goods and horse, and then – a faint misgiving no doubt occurring by this time – avoided Assisi and returned with the money, to pour it out before the poor priest of St. Damian's.

Thus, the new life of universal love began, as new lives of whatever kind are so apt to begin, with a family quarrel. Pietro Bernardone was infuriated. Francis, as his excitement died down, knew what he had to expect and was frightened. He dared not go home, but hid in the neighbourhood of St. Damian's for several weeks. But, obviously, this could not go on. It would be an admission of failure at the outset, a demonstration that his way of taking the world would not work. At last, he came out and went home again – perhaps with still something of the spoilt child's confidence that they would now be so glad to see him, that his crime would be forgotten. But Pietro's rage had reached the sticking-point. He met the prodigal with cuffs and curses and locked him in the cellar, and, when his mother let him out and helped him to escape again, took the cold, ruthless way of the law. Francis appealed to the ecclesiastical courts, though he had no ecclesiastical standing, and the Pilates of Assisi were glad to pass the difficult case on to the bishop. The bishop also, found himself in a difficult position. Francis had effectually passed on his problem. At last, he decided to follow an august precedent, and advised Francis to render unto Caesar the things that were Caesar's, or, in other words, to renounce his family rights. Francis took the words with his usual literalness. Then and there he stripped himself naked, made a pile of his garments and put on top of it all the money that was left. 'Pietro Bernardone is no longer my father,' he announced to the assembled citizens, 'in future, I serve God only.'

Francis's unfortunate parents hardly reappear in any version of the story. Nevertheless, spoilt darlings of a family do not throw away all their worldly prospects without causing some heart-burning. The life of love must have begun by inflicting vital suffering on those who loved the universal lover most.

That Francis himself was morally injured by the violence of the rupture seems clear enough. From this time dates a repulsion for money amounting to an actual, irrational loathing of the coin in itself. His disciples were later forbidden even to touch the filthy abomination – they were to take their alms and their wages for work in kind, if at all. There is an unpleasant story of a brother who picked up a piece of money left by the crucifix of St. Mary Portiuncula and threw it on to the window-sill. Francis made him pick it up with his mouth and carry it to a heap of asses' dung outside. This is a Francis whom one scarcely recognises. But similar stories are too numerous and well authenticated to be rejected.

At this price, Francis Bernardone won his clear start in the new life, with all normal values reversed. He had now completely stripped himself of everything, money, relations, friends, prestige, even literally clothing, except for a peasant's tunic which the bishop had given him in the interests of decency. He could do it, because he lived in Italy. Moral adventures have to be physically possible, or they end abruptly. It was early spring and there were still snowdrifts. If Francis had lived in a northern climate, he would probably have died in a few days. Or, more likely, since he was, after all, a sane man, he would never have attempted the enterprise in that form. He would have had to compromise right at the beginning, as his followers who later came to England had to compromise; and the adventure of the life of love would have lost its clear-cut outline. In Italy, problems and paradoxes came later and more subtly. But Italian sunshine and Italian fertility made the experiment possible.

Francis wandered about the country for a time, singing and rejoicing in his freedom, and then settled down again in a cell at St. Damian's and, money being now out of the question, began to beg bricks and repair the church with his own hands. When that was finished, he passed on to another ruined church and then to another. Meanwhile he lived on scraps that he begged for in the city. At first, some of the normal repulsions survived. At one house, where he went to beg for oil, there was a party going on. The music of it drove Francis away – no doubt, some of his old companions would be there. He had become a figure of fun in the city. Children shouted after him, his own people mocked and mimicked him. But this was a thing that had to be done thoroughly if it were to be done at all. He went back and, when he asked for the oil, proclaimed also to the company his hesitation and the reasons for it.

Outraged senses also revolted sometimes. 'When he

would have eaten that medley of meats, at first he shrank back, for that he had never been used even willingly to see, much less to eat, such refuse.' But when he forced himself to begin, 'it seemed to him that in eating no rich syrup had he ever tasted aught so delicious.'

Fortunately there still remained things that could be loved without such spiritual somersaults – space, air, light, mountains, growings things, creatures. That these might also some day become a perquisite of wealth was unthought of and unthinkable in Francis's day. One wonders whether even he could have made a Troubadour's lady of the poverty of modern cities. Francis's lady was austere, but she had the freedom of the sunshine and the countryside.

Francis was lonely in the two years that followed his conversion. It seemed that the universal lover could expect no personal response. But the poet in him came to the rescue and provided companions. His passion of friendliness spread itself to everything, to the sun and the moon, to all vivid natural objects, to fire and water, birds and animals. These could still be loved without the mental gymnastics which love of one's fellow-men entails. No one had discovered evolution; the struggle for existence was still veiled. A poet could call the birds 'little sisters' and remove worms from his path without any inevitable sense of incongruity. Incongruities, of course, there must have been; but perhaps Francis, who could never have undertaken his adventure at all if he had been a profound logician, still averted his eyes in the old manner when he saw a 'little sister' peck to pieces the worm that he had so carefully removed. Or perhaps he faced the situation, as he had faced his own, and exhorted the worm to die willingly that the little sister might have her breakfast; perhaps he drove the bird gently away, urging her to a vegetarian diet. Brother Juniper, the delightful half-wit, who was like a caricature of Francis, once (according to the *Little Flowers*) cut off a pig's foot, apparently from the living animal, to cook for a sick brother who had expressed a wish for it; and was amazed at the anger of the owner and the reproof of Francis. He could not see 'how there could be any trouble about such an act of charity.' According to the story, Francis's only discomfort seems to have been on the owner's account. But such stories are legendary; they may, or may not, be founded on fact; and they were told by people who were also no logicians. How Francis actually dealt with the discords that even love of sub-human Nature brings in its train must be left to speculation.

The poem of comradeship which is his only written poem must have begun to grow about this time, when 'Brother Fire,' 'Sister Water,' 'our little sisters the swallows' were called in to fill the gap left by the boon companions of Assisi.

Be thou praised, my Lord, through all thy creatures
Especially Sir Brother Sun,
Who brings forth the day and gives thy light,
And he is beautiful and radiant in great splendour
And of Thyself, Most High, is the symbol.

Be thou praised, my Lord, for Sister Moon and the stars,
In the Heaven thou hast formed them, clear and precious and beautiful.

Be thou praised, my Lord, for Brother Wind
And for the air and the clouds and for calm and every weather
Through which thou givest sustenance to all thy creatures.

Be thou praised, my Lord, for Sister Water,
For she is most useful and humble and precious and pure.

Be thou praised, my Lord, for Brother Fire,
Through whom thou lightest up the night
And he is beautiful and gay and vigorous and strong.

Be thou praised, my Lord, for our sister Mother Earth,
Who sustains and nourishes us
And brings forth various fruits and coloured flowers and grass.

These are all beautiful things that can be loved with no more than an expansion of normal consciousness. And here, at first, the poem ended. But the bishop and the mayor of Assisi had quarrelled at that later time when the poem had been written down, and there was added a stanza bringing in the troubled human paradox: –

Be thou praised, my Lord, for those who forgive for thy love,
And endure infirmities and tribulations.
Blessed are they that do suffer in lowliness of spirit
For by thee, Most High, shall they be crowned.

The final addition, composed on Francis's deathbed, gives the last desperate reconciliation: –

Be thou praised, my Lord, for our sister the Death of the Body,
From the which no man can flee;
Grant that those who die may have done no mortal sin.

That human comrades should come in the end to Francis was inevitable, since he had the need of them, and the vital energy that goes for what it needs. Besides, to accept the gospel is to accept also the commission to preach it. A hearing of the passage where the disciples are sent out without gold or money, or scrip, or change of clothing, or shoes, or staff, to give freely what they had freely received, crystallised Francis's impulse to action, and to win the confirmation, which all men, however secure in themselves, crave of their fellows. That the life of love, spread abroad, became in its nature a very different matter from the isolated venture, was outside the range of a mind supremely unphilosophical.

As soon as Francis began to preach, his position in the estimation of the outside world changed. This, the citizens of Assisi understood; the comic lunatic was now behaving in a way they recognised. That Francis was a great orator is evident; but that his sermons would read interestingly, if they survived, improbable. He wrote unwillingly and with difficulty – to be a poet was, in those days, to be a singer, not a writer – and all his written work that remains, apart from the *Hymn of the Sun*, is disappointing. Except for occasional flashes, it is mere imitative ecclesiastical formalities that slide over the mind without gripping. Probably, the substance of the sermons was not very different. One of the few laymen whose comments on Francis remain, said that, though he could remember every word of other men's sermons, Francis's always escaped him, and, if he committed one to memory, it seemed to have changed when he reproduced it. But the words were the least part of Francis's sermons. He preached by gesture, physical and spiritual. One sermon to the Poor Clares consisted solely of the 'Miserere' uttered with such passion that it left the congregation in tears. Another began with a statement which might be freely translated, 'You think me a holy man, but you do not know that throughout this fast I have been eating food cooked with lard.' 'He saw the greatest concourse of people as one man,' says Thomas of Celano, 'and to one man he preached most carefully as if to a multitude.' Sometimes he would forget what he had intended to say and would say so without embarrassment; then, either unpremeditated words would come with a rush, or, if he could think of nothing, he would dismiss the people with his blessing.

The 'advertisement-value' of such methods is obvious, and no doubt Francis was aware of it. To say so, is not to detract from his sincerity. Sincerity is, or should be, a relative term. Francis was an actor, but he was a sincere actor. He was an artist, trying out, with whatever degree of inspiration or of deliberation, a technique of behaviour – in the frank intention of winning men by directness and confidence. And, after he began to preach, he was not long alone.

The first comrade, a wealthy Assisi citizen, Bernard de Quintaville, asked Francis to his house and spent a night talking with him. In the morning, he sold everything he had, gave the money to the poor and built himself a hut at St. Mary Portiuncula, the latest church that Francis had repaired. Several others followed almost at once.

There began the halcyon days of Francis's adventure. To have again like-minded friends after his years of isolation must have been intoxicating to him. And the new brothers threw themselves into the adventure with a delight that indicates what a harassing mental conflict is appeased by Francis's solution. In throwing oneself upon a friendly universe, one shelves in fact an enormous burden of decision. One can put the matter – as with most moral problems and moral solutions – in ignoble as well as in heroic terms. The spoilt child gets rid of his intolerable load of grown-up responsibility in a new way, since he can no longer do it in the old. In Francis's way of life, not merely the moral necessity, but the practical occasions for hesitation, worry and choice were removed.

'If we had any property,' he told the Bishop of Assisi, who protested that their way of living was too hard, 'we should have to defend it and should soon be involved in fighting and disputes and law-suits to the detriment of the love of God and of our neighbour.'

Francis's method with the lusts of the flesh is significant, and the story recurs so frequently and, at the same time, ends so unexpectedly that it is probably true. Once, when so afflicted, he went out into the snow. This is in the true tradition of ascetics who, having found their snow-drift, would then proceed to roll in it. But Francis made himself a number of snow figures. 'This,' he said, addressing his unruly self, 'is your wife; these are your children. Now, you will have to provide for them.' This curiously unecclesiastical treatment of the difficulty seems to have passed Francis's ecclesiastical biographers without comment.

The tramp and gipsy instinct was sanctified in Francis's scheme of life. 'Since they possessed no earthly things, they set their affections on naught, and had naught that they feared to lose; they were everywhere at ease, weighed down by no fear, harassed by no care; they lived like men who were removed from vexations of the mind, and, taking no thought for it, awaited the morrow and their night's lodging.' When Francis was on a missionary journey with a companion and came to a cross-roads, he would tell the other to shut his eyes and turn round. Then they would go in the direction he was facing when he opened them.

The first little community of Brothers at St. Mary Portiuncula reminds one of a camp of schoolboys throwing themselves wholeheartedly into a desert island game. Fun and laughter and humorous exaggeration were in the very penances and hardships themselves. The stories of the *Little Flowers*, especially the antics of Brother Juniper, who gave away everything that anyone left about, convey the spirit of this phase, whether they are all true or not. Francis later banned laughter for his disciples, probably on account of the element of cruelty always present in it, but the brothers of the early days lived many a good joke. One Lord Bishop was surprised to receive a visit in his palace from Brother Francis and Brother Paul and a Sister Sheep whom they had just redeemed from an unhappy fate. A minister who had scolded Brother Juniper until he was hoarse was wakened in the middle of the night to drink some gruel that Brother Juniper had made to cure his hoarseness.

If Francis's own altruism had been no more subtle than this, the game would probably have lasted no longer than such games usually last – until the children were tired of it. It was his personal magnetism that gave such intense vitality to an idea which had only a limited potentiality in itself. The sensitive man who has chosen a life of universal friendship (the ordinary word conveys the meaning best, since 'philanthropy' has suffered the general degeneration of moral terms) attracts love and trust at every turn. He is not a common phenomenon; 'philanthropists' are perhaps more often of the unimaginative type, who are more or less immune to the infection of suffering, but have an organising ability which they laudably wish to apply to useful ends. Francis not only wished to do good to his fellow-men – he felt with them. He was a vain man, and he knew what hurt the vanity in others: he knew jealousy and its agonies and the only way to heal it, as when he told a young Brother who had become morbid in his adoration, that he was dear to him and even among his most beloved, and might come to him at any time – an indulgence for which, no doubt, he had to pay; but then such payment was a part of his vocation. He knew loneliness, too, and how to comfort it without humiliating the outcast. He was the supremely good listener; Chesterton quotes the 'blasphemy': 'He listens to those to whom God Himself will not listen.' And this is a luxury for which poor human nature may well be impelled to surrender every other. Francis listened so well that he sometimes heard even what remained unsaid. There is a story of one of his missionary journeys in which Brother Leo was his companion. Francis, being worn out, was riding on a donkey; and it occurred to Brother Leo that, in the old days, it would have been he that was mounted, for he came of a noble family. The next moment, Francis had dismounted, putting Leo's thought into words. For the companionship of such a man, there will always be people, especially young people, willing to sacrifice home, security, ambition or anything else that may be demanded of them, even without the glamour of a dramatic idea and the relief of escape from the complexities of life.

That it was love of Francis, behind the love of mankind, or love of God, that inspired the early Franciscans becomes clear in the sequel. But, for the moment, it looked as if altruism had indeed got loose on earth. After the first few disciples had come in, the movement began to spread rapidly. It began to lead to complications. The brothers were welcomed in the country, not so welcome in the towns. Young people in the fields threw down their tools and turned and followed them. 'Then it was that the sword which cleaveth asunder was sent upon earth,' says the *Legend of the Three Companions*, 'when the young came into the Religion, leaving their parents in the slough of their sins.'

The first intimations of the paradox of altruism began to appear. Ought everyone to behave in the same way? If the springs of Francis's conduct were right for him, they must be right for everyone. But would they not then lead to the same essential behaviour in everyone? And then what would happen? It is doubtful if Francis ever propounded the problem to himself explicitly; he was an artist, not a philosopher. But the consequences followed none the less. What, in fact, would happen, if we all did it? Suppose we all gave away all our goods and distributed the proceeds to the poor? Suppose we all thought more of other people than of ourselves – deferred to everyone else's wishes and opinions, put their needs before our own, abandoned organised work (which involves denials), ambition, personal desire, material comfort? The answer is easy. Millennium and chaos would come together. Karel Capek has written a romance about a machine for the manufacture of the Absolute (or rather, unbowdlerised, for the manufacture of God), and gives some kind of form to the speculation what would happen if the altruistic instincts of mankind ever could get loose, with normal checks removed. The idea in itself ends in logical absurdity. Even unselfishness would defeat its own ends, and it would become a higher unselfishness to allow other people to do things for one – and so on, in an infinite series, constituting the kind of paradox in which all absolute theories of human thought and conduct must expire. Such abstractions seem removed from practical life. But they have their dim, partial counterparts in practice.

Strong-minded thinkers have, in fact, always been aware of the dangers of extreme altruism, in ordinary so well checked by the self-regarding instinct. It is the basis of the modern reaction against Christianity – of the ruthless superman of Nietzsche set over against the self-abnegating Christ, and of H. G. Wells's godlike men, who had a disgust for pity.

FL

Francis's followers were soon becoming numerous enough to create social difficulties. They clashed with the farmers who did not want their sons to go; they clashed with the parish priests, who did not like their domains invaded by disreputable vagabonds holding revival meetings that must often have seemed more like schoolboy rags than decent religious services. It became obvious, even to Francis, that the thing must obtain some definite recognition and status. Perhaps he even wanted it, for he was still a vain man, though it had become an invertible vanity.

In 1210, he set out to Rome with a little band of followers (that there were precisely twelve is probably a pious fancy) to obtain recognition from the Pope. It is disputed whether he went on his own initiative or pushed by the ecclesiastical authorities, but the logic of facts, in any case, made some such move inevitable. In Rome, the Church looked with some disconcertment at the duckling that it had hatched. There were philosophers among the cardinals. All Francis asked was that the Pope would approve of their decision to live according to the gospel. It seemed a simple and obvious request to make to the Vicar of Christ. But the Vicar of Christ, who was also a sovereign and a statesman, found it anything but simple. There was a flutter in the Curia. The Cardinal of San Sabina, who had been drawn in by the Bishop of Assisi to present Francis's case, put the dilemma in a nutshell. 'If anyone declares that to observe gospel perfection and profess it is an irrational and impossible innovation, is he not convicted of blasphemy against Christ, the author of the gospel?' Innocent III was plainly convinced that, blasphemy or no blasphemy, it was an irrational and impossible innovation, but he could not afford to say so. The Church had got on very well for many centuries by ignoring this particular dilemma. It must have been exasperating to Pope Innocent to have it thrust into his face by a dozen apparently half-crazy beggars from Assisi, who had yet raised a countryside by their ridiculous logic.

Innocent III decided to tame the monster and draw its fangs as and when he could. He tried first to get Francis and his friends into some established Religious Order. It was a crucial point for Francis. Should the movement of self-abnegation carry abnegation to the extent of surrendering its own identity? Even if they were allowed to exist as a special branch of Benedictines, it would not be the same thing – the irresponsibility, the essential amateurishness of the adventure would be gone. It would be as if some hectoring grown-up had come in to organise the Desert Island game. Francis's deference to other people's views was often comic, but he would not defer to the Vicar of Christ in this. What, he asked, could he and his brothers need of rules and formulas beyond the words of Jesus Himself? And, as before, there was no presentable answer.

The Pope gave way for the moment. The brothers received a sort of provisional recognition; he did not think it would work, but they might try for a time. But something had to be done to keep these irresponsible children within bounds. There must be a responsible head who could be called to account, and they must accept the tonsure. The point is more important than it looks at first sight; it was the outward sign not only of Church authority, but that the brothers were set apart from their neighbours – an advertisement that everybody would not be expected to behave like this.

On his return journey, according to one story, though others put it later, Francis received a demonstration of the Holy Father's practical wisdom. A whole village was converted and wanted to rise and follow him. This was too much even for Francis. He and his little band of brothers were gladly fed by the countrymen; but a whole wandering village would strike them rather as an invasion of bandits. A modification of the Rule had to be made, by which members could be as Christian as possible in their own homes and at their own work. It was the germ of the famous Third Order.

In this way, Innocent III inoculated Francis's movement with the anti-toxins of common-sense. They grew with it and eventually killed it. But, for a time, the life of gay haphazard went on, in spite of increasing complications. One of Francis's most surprising adventures occurred soon after the visit to Rome.

It was inevitable that the infection of his idea should spread to the sex that Nature compels to be the more altruistic. Clare was seventeen when she first heard Francis preach and was caught by the glamour. Her family, a noble one of Assisi, was no more pleased than Francis's had been. And Francis dealt with her difficulties as he had dealt with his own. Like a true troubadour, he staged a spiritual elopement. Clare escaped one night from the family mansion with two companions. She went to the Portiuncula, was joyfully received there by torchlight, and took her vows the same night in the presence of Francis and the other brothers. Then they took her to a monastery of friendly Benedictines. Francis was not even in priest's orders and had apparently no authority, but his own, for his actions. That no ecclesiastical censure followed indicates how far the Church had decided to let him have his head. No one, apart from Clare's relations, seems to have made any trouble. They pursued her from monastery to monastery, beat her sister Agnes, when she went to join her, but all in vain. At last, the Benedictines came to the rescue and gave Clare and the companions who came flocking to her, the old Church of St. Damian, which was the first that Francis had repaired. The sisters made their camp there, like the brothers, and lived in poverty, nursing the sick, and helping the poor. Francis's recklessness stopped short of sending them on missionary journeys, but they were regarded as a part of the same community. The brothers returning to the Portiuncula would often bring with them recruits for St. Damian's also.

There appears an odd mixture of recklessness and caution in Francis's treatment of Clare. The problems of sex are certainly crucial for the complete altruist; and Francis's methods with them ought to be particularly illuminating. Unfortunately this issue, more than all others, is obscured by the fact that Francis became a highly honoured saint of the Catholic Church. He was a difficult saint – he caused controversies all his life and after his death. But the Church had undertaken to assimilate him and it did assimilate him. All his biographers were themselves ecclesiastics. It is difficult to guess how far truth – that is, the truth of plain fact – suffered in the process.

Is there any essential reason why sex love should be banned to the complete altruist? It is a difficult question. For sex love is both love and *egoïsme à deux*. Also, to anyone with a universal mission, the universal truth applies: –

> *Down to Gehenna, or up to the Throne,*
> *He travels the fastest who travels alone.*

Yet Francis's inspiration to universal love always remained so much more the sum of impulses of individual sympathy than a thought-out philosophy, that one may suspect that his history in this respect might have been different, if accidents of time and place had not identified his vocation with traditional Christianity and the traditional personality of its founder. 'I may yet have children,' he is reported to have said to his friends at a fairly late stage in his career, and, as no good Catholic is likely to have invented such a remark for a saint, one may take it as authentic. His original treatment of sex temptation has been mentioned. Yet for a man of his intense personal attraction, platonic relations with women must sometimes have involved a coldness and cruelty at odds with his paramount impulse; and there may, therefore, be some truth in the good Churchmen's account of his avoidance of women. One of them goes so far as to say that he would not even raise his eyes to a woman's face. It is also recorded that his own friends once remonstrated with him for cruelly keeping away from the Poor Clares; and how he would send none of the brothers to visit them except those who did not want to go.

There are also other stories quite inconsistent with this picture, in which Francis treated women with his usual gentleness and courtesy. He had apparently a charming friendship with Jacqueline of Settesoli, a Roman lady, whom he called 'Brother Jacqueline,' and to whom he gave a pet lamb that used to call her for Matins. She is said to have come to him on his death-bed, bringing some sweetmeats that he had liked; but this is denied by some clerical writers.

There is also the elopement of young Clare, his constant friendship with her, and recourse to her for advice. To her, also, he went for nursing and reassurance in his sickness. One is inclined to give more weight to the pleasanter stories, both as more in character and as free from the suspicion of propaganda. But, in Francis's peculiar circumstances, they may all be true. For, on this issue, he must have come most hardly up against the paradoxes of altruism – that kindness to one person frequently involves unkindness to another, and that individual benevolence often clashes with general; as well as the behests of the Church and the paramount obligation to self-denial. Even Francis could not solve insoluble problems.

The brothers generally went on struggling with the same problems in their less poignant forms, in the outer world. The worm and the sparrow dilemma constantly recurs in the comings and goings of humanity. Innocent III's recognition had helped the Brothers a little in their dealings with the clergy. But it had not made the clergy like them. No one enjoys a demonstration that he is not equal to his job. Clashes between his brothers and the priests of God distressed Francis acutely. And yet one must spread the Good News at any price. In the official Lives, the greatest emphasis is laid on the saint's humble and devoted attitude towards the official priests of the Church. But such devotion was not always easy. Times were approaching the age of Chaucer with his monk 'full fat and in good point,' and the priests of Gower who went to London 'to sing there for simony, for silver is sweet.' Francis naïvely admonishes his brothers on one occasion to help the clergy, 'cover their lapses, supply their manifold defects, and when you have done so, be the more humble.'

Francis's own way with the problem was characteristic. When the Bishop of Romagna refused him permission to preach in his diocese, saying that he could do all that was necessary himself, Francis went out without a word.

Later he returned and stood there silent. The Bishop asked what he had come back for. 'My Lord,' said Francis, 'when a father has driven a son out of one door, he must come in again by another.' The Bishop was conquered.

But all the brothers had not so completely mastered Francis's technique. Or perhaps the hard reality sometimes pricked through it. They constantly found their work obstructed, and very soon some of them were asking for licenses from the Pope to show to the bishops. The whole spirit of the request was shocking to Francis. He told them that they had misunderstood the Will of God, that they must first convert the bishops by humility and reverence. 'As for me, I desire this privilege from the Lord, that never may I have any privilege from man, except to do reverence to all.'

The brothers who now began to be sent abroad often had a particularly hard time. Those who went first to Germany did not know the language and created a farcical situation by saying 'Ja' to everything that was said to them. This soon developed into tragedy when they said 'Ja' to the question whether they were heretics; and Germany acquired the reputation of a country which only would-be martyrs would wish to visit. There were soon actual martyrdoms in North Africa. To Francis himself, the idea of martyrdom – the ultimate acceptance of the 'bitter for the sweet,' was naturally attractive. In the year after Clare's conversion, 1213, he made his first attempt to reach the Saracens. The Christian world was all on fire with crusading fever. It must have been a horror to Francis, but only one form of protest was possible. He became wildly eager to reach his brothers the Moslems, and convert them by gentler means, or win his martyr's consummation in the attempt. But for this time, he was baffled by wind and water, and forced to continue his mission in Italy and Spain.

But there were by this time brothers who saw no point in unnecessary martyrdom. And that it should be necessary, if they could not win by mere common humanity, was not as clear to them as it was to Francis. Many of them had hardly seen him. Even *The Three Companions* (now supposed to be partly a forgery of the stricter Franciscans) admits that 'they returned with great bitterness of spirit unto the blessed Francis.' By 1218 they had obtained from the Pope the general safe-conduct that they demanded, and this was confirmed by a Bull a year later.

Once admit that privilege and protection are desirable things and Christianity is tamed again. The Church was quick to encourage the new spirit. Cardinal Ugolino, Bishop of Ostia, was soon appointed the guardian of the Order without becoming a member of it himself. Francis himself, had asked for him; had called in this energetic grown-up to organise his game. It had been a bitter struggle. His brothers were suffering; suffering was good; but Francis never brought himself to feel that the unwilling suffering of other people was also blessed; only his own. And his brothers were taking this affliction with bitterness. He wavered (as often – it was another of the unsolved paradoxes of his altruism) between treating them as he treated himself, to whom suffering was welcome, and trying to help their troubles as he helped those of the outside world.

At last, he was moved by a dream of a hen who could not cover her large family of chickens. His appeal to the Pope begins with his usual direct informality:

'My Lord, I have pity for you, by reason of the anxiety and perpetual toil wherewith you must needs keep watch on behalf of the Church of God, and sore ashamed am I that you should have such care and anxiety for us, Brothers Minor . . . Wherefore I do humbly and devoutly beseech Your Holiness that you will deign to grant this Lord Bishop of Ostia to be our Father, that in time of need the brothers may resort unto him, saving alway the dignity of your pre-eminence.'

But there was nothing informal about Ugolino's protectorship. Sabatier makes him the villain of Francis's drama. The real villain was social necessity. Ugolino simply did his job – to make the Franciscans an integral part of the Catholic Church – the Church that has always been so well aware that this sad world needs a good deal more than 'just the art of being kind.' There was much to be done. The Brothers must not be murdered and ill-treated simply because they did not know the language of the people they were sent to; therefore, they must have in scholars. Then, if they all wandered at random, there would be wasteful overlapping in some places and neglect in others. Nor could they always rely on finding a hospitable peasantry, and it would be absurd to die of starvation because people were poor or unfriendly. Also, in so large a number of brothers, there were inevitably a few black sheep and still more fools, and an indiscretion of one would throw disgrace upon all. Therefore, each brother must be responsible to someone, and that someone to someone higher up. They must have a common policy in important matters, and therefore meetings and conferences, and, for those who came to the conferences, houses and churches.

That Ugolino murdered the Franciscan idea by inches in the normal and inevitable course of the work is hardly his fault. The Franciscan idea was made to be murdered – or martyred. Self-abnegation, in the last resort, is suicide. In submitting to the needs of his brothers, in submitting to the will of the Church, Francis himself had denied his own idea. If he had refused to submit, he would have been equally denying it. For submission was its essence.

The rule of 'Obedience' had made a great part of the topsy-turvy charm of that first camp at the Portiuncula. A brother had merely to command another 'on his obedience' to do, or not to do, something and the other must submit. Juniper had once been forbidden 'on his obedience' to give away his tunic and had asked the next beggar he met kindly to take it from him. Francis was sometimes prevented from losing his clothing in the same manner. And not only brothers were to be obeyed; the same submission must be accorded to everyone; 'nor did they make any distinction between the just and the unjust.' What was now to happen when their own friends and appointed masters ordered them to own property and to receive privileges? The latter part of Francis's life was an obstacle race beset with such problems.

His aversion to book-learning was second only to his hatred of money. He had said that when scholars joined the Order they should in some sort strip themselves of their learning, too; it gave them an advantage, and no Brother Minor could possess any advantage. Now, a young novice – for there was now a period of probation – had obtained permission from his Minister to possess a Psalter, but, feeling uncomfortable about it, came to ask Francis if it was all right. Francis went his usual way to work and tried to remove the desire. He compared him to the chroniclers who try to win praise merely by recording the deeds of other people. But the novice still hankered after his Psalter. Francis then told him that he himself had once desired to have books, but had been restrained by the saying of Christ that parables were for others, but direct knowledge for the disciples. The novice was still unsatisfied, and after a long interval came again. Francis told him he should do as his minister directed. The young man turned away, happy, but he had gone only a few steps when Francis ran after him, brought him back and did penance on the spot where he had given the permission.

It was typical of endless dilemmas that now beset Francis's steps. That Ugolino himself had a deep affection for him is clear. 'However disturbed or vexed he might be,' he said, on seeing Francis and talking with him, 'all mental clouds were dispersed, serenity returned, melancholy was put to flight and joy breathed on him from above.' The fact remains that he never gave way to him on any important point, or sacrificed the practical harmony which it was his business to put into the workings of the Order, to the moral harmony that gave Francis his spiritual peace and charm. It must have been a relief to both of them when Francis at last got away on his Saracen adventure in 1219. Ugolino had prevented him from going to France two years before on the grounds that he was needed in Italy. But he seems to have put no obstacle in the way of this other much wilder enterprise. The reasons may have been truly religious; but one suspects that it also crossed the Lord Bishop's mind that, while Francis might create unmanageable situations in Catholic France, there was no harm for him to do among the Saracens.

The failure of the mission is gently covered by the Chroniclers. It achieved neither the conversion of the Saracens, nor Francis's martyrdom. With one companion, he actually penetrated to the presence of the Soldan and received the half-humorous, half-reverential treatment which semi-barbarous races extend to those 'touched by God.' But the Moslem priests would not accept his challenge to trial by fire; the Mohammedan faith 'There is no God, but God; and Mohammed is his prophet,' does not rely on miracles. The Soldan, who understood courtesy, told Francis that while he himself was greatly impressed, his people would never accept a change of faith. He tried in vain to load Francis with presents, showing how little the message had actually got through, and returned him to the Christian camp. Francis, warned by an opportune vision, gave up his attempt. It is not recorded in what language the interview was conducted; but it can hardly have been easy. Francis was no scholar and the Soldan is unlikely to have spoken Italian or French. The personality which was Francis's sole asset would come very inadequately through an interpreter. Like his brothers in Germany, he must have felt the curse of Babel upon the bond of common humanity.

Meanwhile Ugolino had been busy. A month after Francis's departure, the Benedictine rule had been imposed upon the Poor Clares, and they were given various privileges, including the holding of property. About the same time, strict regulations for fasting were drawn up for the Brothers, who had been told, in the First Rule, to eat whatever was set before them; and had been directed by Francis to give 'Brother Ass' enough to keep him from grumbling, though no more. On the other hand, the inherent absurdity in the Franciscan idea had broken out in a strange manifestation. Brother John of Compello had founded an Order of Lepers, male and female, written them a Rule and led them to Rome to obtain the Pope's approval. The Pope took the visitation as might have been expected, but Francis's own comments, which would have been interesting, are not on record.

Francis came back rather as his great prototype had come into the commercialised Temple. He was hailed with delight, for a report of his death had spread universal dismay. But the delight was soon mitigated. At Bologna, on his way from the coast, he found the Brothers in a fine large house that had just been built and was already known as the House of Friars. Next to money, this was the most deadly form of property. It anchored and gave security. Francis was outraged, and for once lost his temper. He ordered the brothers to turn out, not excepting a number of sick. But Ugolino was not far away, and the dismayed brothers ran to him. He hurried to the spot, and assured Francis that the building did not belong to the brothers at all, but was his own property.

There was nothing more that Francis could say. No brother could deny another person's claim to anything. If they took his cloak, he must give his coat also. He went on his way to Assisi with feelings that can be imagined.

It was becoming an impossible situation for a man to whom consistency was all-important. One must give everyone what they want. The Church authorities wanted Francis's Order – his beloved family – and this time he gave it to them completely. At the Chapter of 1220, he resigned the headship of the Order.

'From henceforth am I dead to you,' he told the weeping brothers, 'but behold Brother Peter of Catana whom both I and we all will obey.' And so he commended his 'family' to the Lord, and to its ministers, who would be held responsible for any brother who perished by 'their negligence, or evil example, or bitter correction.'

The last words were ominous. A papal Bull issued eight

days before had denounced severe penalties on friars who transgressed in any way – there was to be no forgiveness for the deserter, and the brother who wandered in the old style, instead of going precisely where he was sent, incurred ecclesiastical punishment until he submitted.

And still, several years later, Francis was writing to Elias, Peter's successor, 'Let there not be a brother in the world who shall have sinned as often as it was possible for him to sin, who, after seeing thy face, shall ever go away without thy pardon, if he seeks pardon. And, if he does not seek pardon, thou shalt ask him if he desires it. And if a thousand times after this he shall appear before your eyes, love him more than me, to the end that thou draw him to the Lord; and always have pity on such.'

But what Francis said no longer mattered. After the 1220 meeting, he was directed to draw up a new Rule for the brothers, incorporating the innovations. With two companions, he went into the mountains to compose it. Bonaventura's, the official Life, says simply and amazingly that, when he returned, he gave it to his Vicar, Elias (the Minister-General was still politely called Francis's Vicar) who 'lost it through negligence.' Another account states frankly that Elias's partisans stole it. Francis retreated again and produced another. It seems likely that he had received certain instructions, 'on his obedience' in the meantime. The Second Rule is sterner than the first on ecclesiastical points of routine; on others it is laxer; the vital provision that the brothers, when they set out on a journey, should take nothing with them, is omitted.

Thus Francis set about resuming his old status of the solitary amateur in the life of Poverty and universal love. He gave up having regular companions, and spent more and more time in lonely retreat in the mountains. But it was not so easy now. He might say that he was dead to them, but it was impossible to dismiss all care for the brothers who still loved him and looked to him. And the new rulers of the Order still needed him as a figure-head, if for nothing else. Francis could no more deny them than he could deny anything else that was asked of him. The tragi-comedy of the man who might not say 'no' went on.

This underground battle between Francis and the development of his own idea is almost hopelessly obscured by ecclesiastical controversy. During his life and for many years after his death, the men who had known him intimately fought a fierce rearguard action for his ideal. The Church could not afford to let the schism have full publicity. All the early biographies are thus controversial, and therefore unreliable. Only reluctant evidence can be accepted as probably true.

Francis could not fight at all without fighting himself. And it was to escape that most terrible of conflicts that he had become what he was. The *Speculum Perfectionis*, now suspected of being in part a forgery of the stricter Franciscans, turns the Francis of the later years into a fulminating Jeremiah, calling down disaster on the Order and on those that have led it astray. To behave like this, Francis must himself have abandoned his whole principle of life. And yet he was in a hopeless dilemma. There must certainly have been sudden, violent flashes of resentment, then repentances and abject recantations, such alternations as in his dealings with the novice who wanted to possess the Psalter.

The mental conflicts, so infinitely more distressing to the religious temperament than any hardship or practical difficulty, were back again. 'What ought I to do?' – to have this question undecided is the one thing intolerable to men who will suffer torture willingly so long as they know the answer.

In one mood, it seemed to Francis that it was the supreme joy that his own no longer accepted him. 'It seemeth not to me that I am a Friar Minor,' he told a friend, 'unless I be in the state which I will tell thee. Behold the friars invite me with great devotion to the Chapter and moved by their devotion I go to the Chapter with them. But they, being gathered together, ask me to announce to them the Word of God and to preach amongst them. And rising up I preach to them as the Holy Spirit shall have taught me. Having finished, therefore, my sermon, put it that all cry out against me, "We will not have thee to reign over us, for thou art not eloquent, as is becoming, and thou art too simple and idiotic, and we fear greatly to have so simple and despised a superior over us, whence, henceforth, presume not to call thyself our prelate !" And so they cast me out with blame and reproach. It would seem to me that I was not a Friar Minor, if I did not rejoice to the same extent when they reproached me and cast me out with shame, unwilling that I should be their prelate, as when they venerate and honour me.'

This passage is from the suspect *Speculum*, which does not err on the side of submissiveness. On the other hand, Thomas of Celano, whose *Life* was commissioned by the authorities, records a flash from Francis's sick-bed, 'Who are they that have snatched the Religion of myself and the brethren out of my hands? If I get to the Chapter-General, then I will show them what my will is !'

Thomas of Celano wrote his second *Life* after the disgrace of Elias, who had gone too far even for the Church, making the Franciscan Friars a close and wealthy syndicate with himself as autocratic head. In the reaction, something of Francis's antagonism was allowed to come through, though not enough to cause real scandal. In general, Celano has only vague passages about Francis's unhappiness over weak and backsliding brothers and evil examples, giving, except in that one dramatic flash, no names or places.

But there was, and could be, no open breach in Francis's lifetime. Francis was too eager for the reality, and the Church for the appearance of peace and concord.

Sometimes he tried his old remedy of the refusal to see. He would often go away, says the same biographer, 'lest he might chance to hear anything unfavourable concerning any one of them, to the renewing of his grief.' He told Peter of Catania to put down scandal-mongering with severe punishment. 'Hand him over to the Florentine bruiser if thou canst not punish him thyself.' The 'Florentine bruiser' was John of Florence, the Hercules of the Order.

And sometimes things still seemed to go with the old delightful insouciance. The famous Chapter of 1221 was full of gaiety and good will. The people of Assisi and the countryside had provided so abundantly for the brothers that they had to stay two extra days to eat everything up, although there were 2,000 of them. Brother Francis sat at the feet of Elias, his Vicar, and pulled his tunic when he wanted to speak. Volunteers for dangerous Germany were called for.

'Brethren,' said Elias, speaking for Francis, 'thus saith the Brother; there is a certain land named Germany, in which there are devout Christian men. These, as ye know, often go through our land with long staves and great candles, sweating in the sun's heat, singing praises to God and his Saints, and visit the shrines of the Saints.'

Brother Jordan, with true Franciscan humility, tells a good story against himself on this occasion. He had a Boswellian passion for getting details of any brothers likely to do great things, and especially of potential martyrs. He hurried among the ninety volunteers and began to take down their names. A jovial brother collared him and held him there. Meanwhile, he was assigned to another province. But Brother Caesar of Speyer, choosing among the ninety, soon discovered the involuntary volunteer and he was hauled before Elias. Elias told him to choose for himself. Poor Jordan, wavering between pride and fear, consulted a Brother who had fifteen times lost his breeches in Hungary, and was advised to leave it to Elias. Elias included him in the mission to Germany; and it is pleasant to know that he survived to write the story; for, this time, the German mission included scholars who could speak German, Lombard and Latin.

Yet it was this same Elias at whose feet Francis was sitting, who became the Judas of the story to the stricter Franciscans. He was a self-educated man, who had begun first as artisan and then as schoolmaster in Assisi, and later became a lawyer in Bologna. Such a rise was a great achievement in those days and Elias was said to be the greatest master of human wisdom in all Italy. There is no record to show why and how he joined the Order of 'little poor men,' but he had made a great success of a mission to Syria and had come back with Francis after his journey to the Saracens. Sabatier makes a romance of his relations with Francis. There is a shadowy story that Francis had had some un-named companion and confidant during the two years of moral suffering which preceded his conversion; and the Frenchman, who so strongly felt the romantic side of Francis's life that he made his relations with Clare into a sort of transcendental love-story, has also imagined that this companion was Elias, on no other grounds than that he also was a citizen of Assisi, about Francis's age, and that it was no one else who can be identified. This, he believed, was why Francis showed so much forbearance and even affection for the man who most of all distorted his ideas; whose understanding, or sympathy, was so small that he began building a magnificent cathedral in Francis's honour as soon as he was dead, taxing the brothers to provide the funds. The explanation may or may not be true – the chances seem against it. In any case, it is unnecessary. Francis's relations with Elias, in the nature of the case, must have been what psychologists have taught us to call 'ambivalent.' Elias was Ugolino's man, a scholar, an organiser, an ambitious administrator. He was also a brother, Francis's Vicar, the head of the 'little poor men,' 'simple and idiotic', of Assisi, and to him, above all others, was due love and submission. He must, for Francis, have been the very crux and symbol of his alternating love and anger.

Elias, too, like everyone else, probably had an affection for Francis. In spite of the later blackening of his character when he had offended the Church itself, there are pleasant stories of their relationship. No doubt the truth is that he was a genuine philanthropist, but one of the other kind – the one who wishes to do good and to do it in his own way, *de haut en bas*; and, therefore, far more difficult to deal with than a direct enemy.

But Francis had passed the point when he could attempt to deal with anything. The Order was out of his hands, not to be enticed back by any of the gentle coaxing which was his only weapon. When organisation comes in, friendliness goes out. He lived on several years, still an amateur in the life of poverty, often a recluse, sometimes coming and going among the brothers – for no one yet tried to regulate his comings and goings. His obsession with the Passion of Jesus became more and more marked as his own moral crucifixion proceeded. His health had been failing ever since the Palestine journey – the trouble, as might be expected, seems to have been digestive. And now, under stress of continual weeping, his eyesight began to go. When the doctor advised him to restrain his tears, he told him that that would extinguish the light of the spirit. In 1224, after a crisis of mystic agony, appeared the marks of nails in his hands and feet and a wound in his side, of whose reality, whatever cause is assigned for it, there appears to be no reasonable doubt.

After this, Francis was sickening for his death, and rejoicing in it. His mind became clearer and therefore happier. The burden of doubt and decision was again passing away from him; whatever happened now, he could do no more. From his disappointment with men, he turned again to things and creatures. He composed the Hymn of Brother Sun and was always singing it. When they cauterised his eyes, he addressed the glowing irons, 'Brother Fire, you are beautiful above all creatures, be kindly to me now; you know how much I have always loved you, now be courteous to me to-day.' Modern cynicism is apt to find Francis sentimental. But it is difficult to laugh at this particular display of sentimentality.

About Francis's lingering illness and deathbed is a strangely ironic atmosphere of relief and rejoicing – and not only the relief and rejoicing of the man himself who was approaching his climax of abnegation, but of others also. It was partly, no doubt, sympathy with his own spirit. Suffering was the proper thing for a saint. To the religiously minded, his refusal to cease the weeping which was bringing blindness, so repugnant to modern ideas, seemed rather as the martyrdom of X-ray experimenters seems to us. He was giving up a lesser value for a greater. But the exaltation was double-edged. This particular saint would certainly now be more valuable dead than alive. Even now, Francis had sometimes abrupt reactions from the atmosphere that surrounded him. He had sudden impulses – to return to the lepers and 'be held in contempt as he had once been,' or to retreat into some remote cave and be seen no more. When he was excited by the *Hymn of the Sun*, he even thought of starting a new Order among the brothers, an order to be led by Brother Pacifico, the poet, who would go singing it about the country and be called the *Jongleurs de Dieu*. If Francis had not lived so fast and had not been old at forty, he might yet have given the Church more exercise. But he had no longer the vitality for a fresh breakaway. He was handed round helplessly as a sort of fetish. Four brothers devoted themselves to looking after him. The authorities wanted him again now that he was dying – as a sacred mascot.

When his illness took a serious turn at Siena, six months before his death, Elias rushed to the spot and began to convey him as rapidly as possible to Assisi. Francis himself wished to die there, and the Assisi citizens were determined that he should. They sent formally appointed armed messengers to demand the delivery of his person, 'that they might not, as touching the Man of God's body, " give their glory to another ".' Thomas de Celano describes the band of Knights 'reverently bringing him home on horseback.' When Francis's body, still living, though the doctors wondered that such a bag of skin and bone could still hold the spirit, reached his native place, 'the city rejoiced . . . and the mouths of all the people praised God, for the whole multitude hoped that the holy man might soon die, and this was the matter of their so great exultation.'

Francis, who wished to die at the Portiuncula, was taken to the Bishop's Palace and guards were set around it.

Elias was concerned that all should be in due order. He remonstrated with Francis because the palace resounded with singing, which might cause scandal among the guards and citizens. Francis refused to modify his welcome to his Sister, the Death of the Body. Perhaps this was why, in the end, they carried him to the Portiuncula, after all.

There, Francis dictated his Testament. 'When the Lord gave me friars, no one showed me what I must do, and the Most High revealed to me that I must live according to the rule of the Holy Gospel. And I caused it to be written in few and simple words and the Lord Pope confirmed it. And those who came to embrace this life gave as much as they could to the poor; they were content with a single tunic patched within and without at will, with the cord and the breeches. And we wished for no more.' Then it tells the brothers all over again, as if nothing had passed in the last ten years, that they are not to accept churches or dwellings, 'unless they are as is becoming the holy poverty' and that they are never to ask for credentials in any form.

Francis was incorrigible. Even on his deathbed he still tried to combine incompatibles. The Testament proceeded with a declaration of absolute obedience to the Minister-General of the Brotherhood, and in the last paragraph binds him and all other authorities, 'on their obedience,' not to add or take from it, but to let it be kept and read with the Rule, 'And I strictly command all my friars, clerk and lay, not to put glosses on the Rule, nor on these words, saying; "Thus must they be understood." '

Thus he adjured his official superiors 'on their obedience' not to do what they would certainly wish to do and had, in fact, already done. But Francis was passing beyond the persecution of paradox. He died on October

3rd, 1226, and was buried in the big city church inside the walls, lest his body should be stolen. Some two years later, he was canonised by Ugolino, now Pope Gregory IX, and, two years after that, the brothers were told by Papal Bull that they were not bound by the Testament. But some of them still thought that they were; and Bernard de Quintaville, the first disciple, whom Francis on his deathbed had charged Elias 'to love and honour as myself,' was presently hiding in the mountains, hunted by the brothers of the 'Common Observance.' Francis, of the uncommon observance, had died in good time.

ACKNOWLEDGMENTS

In Section II, quotations from the translation of *The Legend of St. Francis by the Three Companions*, published by Dent, are on pages 45, 64, 73, 73–74; from the translation of *The Life of St. Francis by St. Bonaventura*, published by Dent, on page 62, lines 17–23; from the translation of *Speculum Perfectionis*, published by Dent, on page 72, lines 14–16, and pages 78, 81; from the translation of the *Chronicle of Brother Jordan*, published by Dent, on page 82, lines 26–31; from the translation of the *Lives of St. Francis by Brother Thomas of Celano*, published by Methuen, on pages 50, 52, 60, 71, 72, line 2, pages 76, 81, 82, 86; from the translation of the *Writings of St. Francis of Assisi*, published by Burns and Oates, on page 87.

The writer also wishes to thank Miss Jean Murray for her kind assistance in making the close translation of the *Hymn of Brother Sun*, on pages 58–9.

In Section II the quotations on pages 66 and 85 are original translations from Sabatier's *Vie de Saint François d'Assise*, and that on page 79 is an original translation from E. Lempp's *Frère Elie de Cortone*. Other translations already referred to are original.

III

THE MAN OF THE WORLD

A MAN can very well get through life without thinking much about his relations with the universe in general. If he is born into a highly artificial society, in which he has a recognised position, and if he is of an active, creative turn of mind, he may well find scope enough for his imagination and his talents in making the best of the medium that is offered to him. It is a frame of mind that most moderately successful people seem to develop in middle-age. The rebellious ideas of youth have been battered, quenched, ridiculed, coaxed out of existence. This society of human beings that has grown up through centuries by an inextricable mixture of chance and purpose proves to be enormously strong. Short of genius, one can make one's mark on it only by accepting it; one will do most, by going further in the direction in which it is already moving.

A youth of clear head and cool sympathies learns all this earlier than his contemporaries. He sees that his relations with his fellow citizens are going to be all-important to him. But, being after all still young, he must take up his stand with something of a flourish, and follow his line vigorously and definitely. A scheme of social behaviour is his first necessity.

In the eighteenth century, in Western Europe, existed that nucleus of people, leisured, of assured position, above financial anxiety, with opportunities for education and mutual intercourse, such as Clive Bell has described in his illuminating essay, as the first essential for Civilisation.

Its centre was, of course, in Paris, but privileged individuals of all European nations might and did belong to it. Intellectual curiosity, tolerance, the disciplining of jealousy and malice, which accompanies such flowerings of the Spirit of Urbanity, precluded any barriers of patriotism. Eighteenth century Europe was rent by frequent wars, but friendly intercourse between the cultured subjects of the belligerent countries continued with no breaks except those caused by material difficulties. Such outbursts as those in which German and English professors indulged between 1914 and 1918 would have been a subject for shocked laughter in Paris salons, even perhaps in the better-class coffee-houses of London.

This cultured nucleus had its own morality, which was not the morality of the Puritans. Its standard was 'decency' in the old classical sense – that is, satisfactory and graceful behaviour towards one's fellows. It is an ideal that can be made very inclusive. The toning down of one's own egotisms, the tactful consideration of other people's, with the help of rationality, art and humour – this can well be brought to cover the whole duty of man. The person with completely good manners is one of whom no more can reasonably be demanded.

The Paris salons had developed their own technique in this art of living and created a spiritual climate – the climate which, dispersed in the cataclysm of the Revolution, Burke lamented in terms so shocking to some of his fellow-countrymen – 'That unbought grace of life . . . which ennobled whatever it touched, and under which vice itself lost half its evil, by losing all its grossness.'

It is a charm difficult to realise in our own Age, when the business of moneymaking is all-important and all-pervading – this artistry of perfection in human relationships.

A lubberly youth, raw from the University, but to whom to be a completely civilised man seemed the end of existence, descended upon the Paris salons in 1714, set upon learning his manners in the best school. He already knew very well what he wanted; he merely, as he put it himself, 'aimed at perfection,' as exemplified in 'people of shining rank and character.' He had the backing necessary for the enterprise. He was of an aristocratic and sufficiently wealthy English family, heir to its title, with the connections required to start him well among the governing classes of his country. He had also the kind of handicap that acts as an additional stimulus. He was plain to ugliness and had an awkward figure. 'A person as disagreeable as it was possible for a human figure to be without being deformed . . . very short, disproportioned, thick and clumsily made; a broad, rough-featured, ugly face and black teeth and a head big enough for a Polyphemus . . . a stunted giant.' This was an enemy's description; but even a eulogist could only say 'A slight made man of middle size, rather genteel than handsome either in face or person.' In his old age, Chesterfield showed a pathetic anxiety about the physical development of his godson and heir. 'I have now some hopes,' he wrote to the child's father, 'of his rising above the ridiculous Stanhope standard.'

That word 'ridiculous' contains the small tragedy of Chesterfield's own appearance in society. It made it 'an uphill game,' for him, as he later confessed to his handsome, but boorish, young son. But, ugly and awkward as he was, the youth tackled Paris. He describes his *début*, in terms which make one feel that life on a desert island might well be a more comfortable enterprise.

'I was frightened out of my wits. I was determined to

be what I thought civil. I made fine low bows and placed myself below everybody, but when I was spoken to, or attempted to speak myself, *obstipui steteruntque comae et vox faucibus haesit.* If I saw people whisper, I was sure it was at me; and I thought myself the sole object of either the ridicule or the censure of the whole company . . .

'I got more (courage) soon afterwards and was intrepid enough to go up to a fine woman, and tell her that I thought it a warm day; she answered me, very civilly, that she thought so, too, upon which the conversation ceased, on my part, for some time; till she, good-naturedly resuming it, spoke to me thus, "I see your embarrassment and I am sure that the few words you said to me, cost you a great deal, but do not be discouraged for that reason, and avoid good company. We see that you desire to please; and that is the main point; you want only the manner, and you think that you want it still more than you do. You must go through your novitiate before you can profess good-breeding; and if you will be my novice, I will present you to my acquaintances as such."

'You will easily imagine how much this speech pleased me and how awkwardly I answered it. I hemmed once or twice (for it gave me a bur in my throat) before I could tell her that I was very much obliged to her; that it was true; that I had a great deal of reason to distrust my behaviour, not being used to fine company, and that I should be proud of being her novice and receiving her instructions. As soon as I had stumbled out this answer, she called up three or four people to her and said . . . "Do you know that I have undertaken this young man, and he must be encouraged? You will assist me in polishing him. As for me, I believe I have made a conquest of him; for he just now ventured to tell me, though tremblingly, that it is warm. He must necessarily have a passion for somebody, and if he does not think me worthy of it, we will find him another . . ." '

The lady's treatment of the situation with its piquant combination of frankness, provocativeness and friendliness is a fine example of the technique which young Stanhope longed to master, and which, so far as such a thing can be learnt, in time he mastered perfectly. Socrates spent his life asking 'Can virtue be taught?'; Chesterfield might well have spent his asking 'Can the art of pleasing be taught?' But, in that case, he would have remained a philosopher, and not an experimenter in conduct.

His patroness evidently agreed with him that the desire to please was a long step towards doing so, without making any distinction between a rational and an instinctive desire. It was a rational age, and Chesterfield was one of the most rational men who lived in it. He himself expressed the belief that a man could become anything he chose, 'except a good poet.' His whole life is a comment on the theory as applied to social success.

The Paris salons crystallised young Stanhope's ideas for him and many years later, his ideal man was still 'a cultured Frenchman.' But he learnt his business from the bottom up. He was systematic. 'I studied attentively and minutely,' he tells his son, 'the air, the manner, the address and turn of conversation of all those whom I found to be people in fashion and most generally allowed to please. I imitated them as well as I could; if I heard that one man was reckoned remarkably genteel, I carefully watched his dress, motions and attitudes and formed my own upon them. When I heard of another whose conversation was agreeable and engaging, I listened and attended to the turn of it . . . My passion for pleasing was so strong, that I own to you fairly, I wished to make every woman I saw in love with me and every man I met, admire me . . . I always dressed, looked and talked my best, and I own I was overjoyed whenever I perceived that by all these or by any one of them, the company was pleased with me.'

He confesses to a few mistakes. The letters to his son and his godson many years later give the history and philosophy of his experience. He was so determined to be adaptable that he 'borrowed vices.' He drank, though he disliked it and it made him ill, because he thought drinking a 'necessary qualification for a man of pleasure and a fine gentleman.' He took to gambling for the same reason and continued it, even though he presently came to perceive that 'a real man of fashion and pleasure observes decency; at least, neither affects nor borrows vices; and if he unfortunately has any, he gratifies them with choice, delicacy and secrecy.' Yet the gambling habit fastened permanently upon Chesterfield. There is an odd story that he once warned a young nobleman against playing with certain gamesters at Bath and was later found playing with them himself. Perhaps this incessant impulse to throw himself upon chance may be taken as the one necessary compensation of a life consecrated to rational purpose and self-restraint.

Through the greater part of his long life Chesterfield's spiritual home remained the Paris salons. There he was *décrotté* – that favourite word which he translates in the vocabulary of fashion that he made for little Philip Stanhope as 'polished,' though the harsh French original suggests rather 'scoured.' He became so completely master of the language that, in his old age, he was made a member of the Academy. In his correspondence, he drops into French wherever possible, and his graceful periods, his caressing compliments, which sometimes sound affected in English, take on at once their fitting garments. In writing, at least, he had caught the idiom perfectly. In the 'minuet time' that he was always recommending to his young clodhopper, he sends a young fellow-country woman many years later to visit Mme. de Tencin, a lady of the salons, who may, indeed, have been the very person who gave him his own first lesson. He has hesitated long before daring the attempt, he tells her, but desire both to oblige a lady who deserves it and to resume a connection so precious to him has overcome discretion. It would be a poor return for what he owes his correspondent, to push upon her those of his compatriots who are not formed for society and would be out of place in her *milieu*; but Mme. Cleland is English only by birth, and French by regeneration. She has chosen him for her introducer because, like other travellers, he has boasted of his associations with distinguished personalities, and even, if possible, exaggerated Mme. de Tencin's kindness to him: and now his effrontery meets with its just reward. . . .

Mme. de Tencin returns the ball gallantly. She has read Chesterfield's letter to some company. 'What you say as a flatterer restrained me a few moments from showing it, but one's *amour propre* always finds a means to have its way. Mine suggested to me that it would be an injustice to deprive you, under the pretext of modesty, of the applause that was your due.' The company, however, had been chagrined. They protested bitterly against this Englishman who, not content with his supremacy in his own country, dared to write French better than they could themselves. A note enclosed from Fontenelle warns Chesterfield to beware how he arouses the jealousy of French authors.

The acquirement of the perfect manner in speech and

personal intercourse was probably more arduous and its results more doubtful. A style in personal behaviour is as indispensable to the self-conscious as a style in writing; also infinitely more difficult. One meets them everywhere – shy people who have been forced to go into society, and have formed a protective armour of breeziness, of silent mysteriousness, of embarrassing cordiality, or of witty cynicism. In writing, a clever man can usually make his manner convincing; there are no disconcerting interruptions, no unexpected incidents, no irreverent comments. In personal intercourse, it is nearly always transparent, at least, to the more subtle observers; and always it is eclipsed by the gay charm of spontaneous good-will; even the shy man who remains frankly shy is apt to get more mercy and more genuine liking. Chesterfield probably brought this artificial achievement of a manner, this politeness of the head, to the greatest success of which it is capable. And yet people always knew that it was artificial. He was distrusted and he was, after all, easy to disconcert; he could attack vigorously, but defend only weakly, says one of his critics. He even bored people at times. A crony of Lady Denbigh's, anticipating a dull party, writes that she knows so well what will happen from four to eleven.

'Lord Chesterfield will say some epigrams, his good wife and your sister will say almost nothing, my neighbour will utter follies to which Mr. Cook and Southcote will reply with *quolibets* that Lady Jane will raise with her good sense and prudish air, whilst in a corner of the room Lady Charlotte and her good friend will indulge in a little scandalous tête-à-tête; tea, cards, candles and I, we shall do the honours.'

Nevertheless, so far as it could be learnt, young Stanhope learnt the pretty game of the French salons. For him, it was the training that precedes the fight. He was not learning to deal with men and women merely in order to become the complete lounge lizard. He intended to shine in a wider sphere. His chance came before he was quite ready for it, when he would gladly have spent another year wandering about the courts of Europe, finishing what Paris had so well begun. But his great-uncle, General Stanhope, had now become Secretary of State to the new King from Hanover, George I, and the opportunity offered to begin that career of courtier-politician, which was then the recognised ladder for ambitious young aristocrats. The novice hurried home from his schooling to become Gentleman of the Bedchamber to the Prince of Wales and to enter the House of Commons.

So began Philip Stanhope's long and turbulent association with the German gentleman, eleven years his senior, who was to have more influence on his career than any other individual. It seemed an excellent opening. The Prince had a miniature court where a young knight in the art of pleasing could practise his first tilts and break his first lances. Prince George, as the *preux chevalier* for such a tilt-yard, perhaps left something to be desired, however. He was a typical member of his family, and the House of Hanover did not come from, and had never passed by way of, Paris. They did not make a fine art of living. They were Teutonic in their habits. They were folk who had prejudices and who expressed them. They took violent likings and dislikes. They might have been taken as a model family by the Freudian school which believes most of the manifestations of life to be based on the antipathy of father and son; so that, if one pleased one of them, one could be fairly certain of displeasing another at the same moment.

When the King and the Prince quarrelled about the choice of a godfather for the Prince's son, and the quarrel developed into a feud, everyone was forced to take sides. If young Stanhope would come over to the King, he was told, his father should have a dukedom. Young Stanhope disliked his father (though, unlike his master, he kept up appearances) and he did not think the family fortune would support a dukedom. More important, was it better to offend the Fount of Honour, or the Heir-Apparent, who was also his immediate patron? George I was already elderly. Stanhope decided in favour of the Prince.

It turned out to be a mistake. George I lived another ten years, and the career of everyone connected with the Prince was held up in the meantime. No one, of course, suspected that the delay would last so long and Stanhope devoted his time to consolidating his position with the Heir and to cultivating such graces as were to be found in English society. He became a member of the coterie of literary men and cultured young politicians that centred round Pope at Twickenham. It seemed a fortunate accident that Henrietta Howard, the Prince's mistress, also had literary leanings and a taste for the game of graceful badinage. There appeared to be no possible pitfall in such a friendship. The Princess of Wales, a woman of brains and character, who, with her ally, Walpole, was later to rule England for some fifteen years, displayed a truly civilised complaisance towards her husband's liaison – Mrs. Howard was one of her own maids of honour. It never occurred to young Stanhope, fresh from the established tolerance of Paris, that this complaisance might be no more than on the surface. It occurred to other people, however. The Walpoles, who were in the best position to know, gave his friendship with Mrs.

Howard as the root reason why the most accomplished of the Prince's courtiers did not reap the reward of his loyalty when the Prince at last succeeded. For, though he loved his mistress, the Prince went for advice to his clever wife.

Unconscious of his doom, Stanhope took the period of probation with sufficient grace. He could not forge ahead with his political career, but he could create his position in society. One hears little of him at this time, compared with the vast amount of applause and criticism that was poured upon him in the later years when his personality was established in the public eye. But it must have been during this phase that he gradually built up that personality.

'In company with men,' he tells his son, 'I always endeavoured to outshine, or, at least, if possible, to equal the most shining man in it. This desire elicited whatever powers I had to gratify it; and, where I could not perhaps shine in the first, enabled me at least, to shine in the second or third sphere. By these means I soon grew in fashion; and when a man is in fashion, all he does is right.

'It was an infinite pleasure to me to find my own fashion and popularity. I was sent for to all parties of pleasure, both of men and women; where in some measure, I gave the *ton*. This gave me the reputation of having had some women of condition, and that reputation, whether true or false, really got me others. With the men, I was a Proteus, and assumed every shape in order to please them all; with the gay, I was the gayest; among the grave, the gravest; and I never omitted the least attentions of good breeding, or the least offices of friendship, that could either please or attach them to me – and, accordingly, I was soon connected with all the men of fashion or figure in town.'

That Chesterfield formed the connections he claimed is evident; that the nature of those connections was exactly what he imagined it to be, less so. One of the most vivid pictures of him that has come down is that of Lord Hervey – the gentleman about whom he made the *bon mot*, 'At the beginning God created three different species – men, women and Herveys.' Lord Hervey's view of Chesterfield was somewhat different from Chesterfield's own, 'A more conversable table-wit than any man of his time; his propensity for ridicule in which he indulged himself with infinite humour and no distinction and with inexhaustible spirits and no discretion, made him sought and feared, liked and not loved, by most of his acquaintance. No sex, no relation, no rank, no power, no profession, no friendship, no obligation was a shield from those pointed glittering weapons.'

Hervey gives him as the typical example of Boileau's lines:

> *Mais c'est un petit fou qui se croit tout permis,*
> *Et qui, pour un bon mot, va perdre vingt amis.*

Hervey's account is, of course, prejudiced; but what was this paladin in the art of pleasing about, to create such a prejudice in the mind of a man of standing and influence – a prejudice which was emphatically shared by many others? One sees, however, Chesterfield's difficulty. Is the agreeable companion one who is agreeable to everyone, or one who is agreeable about everyone? No one can live a sociable life very long without coming to the painfully uncivilised conclusion that the surest cement for friendship is still common enmities, even as the most interesting small-talk is about the foibles and failings of other people. Whether or not those psychologists are right who put the 'survival value' of a sense of humour as a wholesome reaction from undue sympathy, the element of cruelty in it seems to be inherent. Chesterfield tried to shine in society by being witty; and to be witty in society about the absent is not always to be discounted by charm in their presence – these things get round. And Chesterfield's English contemporaries were hardly civilised enough to find the glory of having provoked a *bon mot* sufficient balm for the impact of the *bon mot* itself.

Chesterfield himself, who so forthrightly confessed his gambling follies and his profligacy to the son who was to profit by his mistakes, never owned explicitly that he had made many and bitter enemies. That was too near a touch. But there is a sentence that occurs almost as frequently in his letters of instruction as the eternal *décrotter* itself.

'An injury is sooner forgiven than an insult.' Again and again it recurs in almost identical words like the touch of the tongue on a sore tooth. At last, when he has passed on to the training of his young heir, he has become doubtful whether it is worth while to be witty at all. 'My dear little boy, if God gives you wit, which I am not sure that I wish you, unless He gives you at the same time, at least an equal portion of judgment to keep it in good order, wear it like your sword in your scabbard, and do not brandish it to the terror of the company. . . . The more wit you have, the more good nature and politeness you must show to induce people to pardon your superiority; for that is no easy matter.'

He who makes no enemies will, however, make nothing else. Chesterfield made himself a fine gentleman, but not according to his own idea of one, as a man who is *persona grata* to everyone. The scheme worked in a vicious circle.

One cannot excel in society without being amusing; one can rarely be amusing except at someone's expense; one cannot be amusing at others' expense without making enemies.

Is a gentleman one who 'is never rude unintentionally', or one who is never rude at all? The later Chesterfield of the Letters held the latter opinion so strongly that he almost worked round to the Christian ideal – always to do as you would be done by; but, if the earlier Chesterfield had acted upon it, he would hardly have cut the figure that he did. His manner, indeed, was always impeccable. As Colley Cibber said in his eulogy, 'His sharpest replies were always polite.' But can a sharp reply ever be fundamentally polite?

Then there were the other difficulties of synthetic charm of manner. It requires a special audience. And English people generally were not familiar with the technique of the Paris salons. Young Stanhope's early efforts in the House of Commons were only too well appreciated, just as the 'Oxford manner' is appreciated at a meeting of North-country miners. Still more so, were the efforts of his mimic. Later, he tells his young hopeful how to take a joke against himself – to pretend that he does not see that it is intended for him, if at all possible; or, if it is unmistakeable, to join in the laugh with apparent good-humour. There is no special recipe, however, to meet the peculiar difficulties of taking mimicry well in public, and, in the House of Commons, the future Lord Chesterfield fell silent, until the welcome death of his father transferred him to a more select audience. There, he soon made a reputation for fine oratory in prepared and declaimed speeches; he was always, apparently, regarded as useless in debate.

When George I died at last, one of the first actions of his

successor was to get rid of Chesterfield. It had, of course, to be an honourable shelving. He was made a Privy Councillor, and, at the same time, appointed ambassador at the Hague. It was just good enough not to be an insult; the position had some diplomatic importance, since the Netherlands was likely to be a balancing factor in any war that might break out – and wars were always either imminent or raging in eighteenth-century Europe.

But it was a blind alley for anyone desiring high political honours. Chesterfield took his exile with outward grace, and behind the scenes worked desperately for his recall.

He did not know until he left it how well, in fact, his situation at the Hague suited him. It was a small framework, a limited society, not too sophisticated, but cosmopolitan enough to admire sophistication. Chesterfield had an assured and independent position. There was his own little court, his equerry, his chaplain, his subordinate officials, including even a poet, Hammond, who alternated between spasms of solitary composition and shining sociability, and was very congenial to his chief. There was opportunity for patronage – always an agreeable preoccupation to Chesterfield. Then there were his equals, the ambassadors of other powers, with whom to play the delicate game of diplomacy. Chesterfield played it in first-class style. It was a field in which conscious adaptability can make a shining success. Spontaneity in responsible men negotiating for their countries with others of different race and language is not expected and would hardly be approved. The language of diplomacy is French. Chesterfield managed well the complications caused by the savage and irresponsible King of Prussia; he prepared the way for a royal marriage, making himself the patron of young William of Orange, the future

Statholder. One sees a premonition of the inveterate former of youth in his report on the young prince. 'He is perfectly well-bred and civil to everybody, with an ease and freedom that is seldom acquired but by a long knowledge of the world. His face is handsome; his shape not so advantageous as could be wished, though not near so bad as I had heard it represented.' He even won the King's gratitude, and there was a hurried, confused intrigue following the royal passage from Hanover in 1730, when Chesterfield visited London and was expected to remain as Secretary of State, but finally retired to the Hague again, expressing himself more than satisfied with the Order of the Garter and the sinecure of the Lord Stewardship of the Household.

Outside of business, there was a lively little social circle at the Hague, when the morning's work was done – the promenade, the gaming-rooms, the drawing-room flirtations, the dances and parties of quadrille. Altogether it was a manageable little world for a man in his early thirties who had at last formed himself according to his own specifications and now wanted a sphere for practising his talents. Chesterfield made a brilliant success in it, and, when he returned to England, brought back the prestige of one who has succeeded in impressing foreigners even more than his own fellow-countrymen.

There had, however, been a payment to make for the achievement. He brought back something else than prestige from the Hague, and left something even more vital – most of his fortune on the gaming tables.

The Hague had its Puritans as well as its cosmopolitans. One of them had been Mlle. du Bouchet, an exiled Frenchwoman, who acted as *Dame de Compagnie* to young Dutch girls of good family. The story, first told, without any authority given, in the Quarterly Review of 1845, is that Mlle. du Bouchet had displayed the strongest aversion to Chesterfield on account of his reputation as a Don Juan, and had ostentatiously hustled her charges away whenever he came within range. It was a challenge that a Man of the World could hardly ignore. Chesterfield made a bet that he would seduce first the lady herself and then the handsomest of her pupils. The first part of the programme, at least, was carried out, and the prude soon found herself about to become the mother of her *bête noir's* child. The episode (which may very well, however, have been dramatically touched up) seems to be in a rather fiercer measure than the 'minuet time' that Chesterfield always recommended. His own comment on it, when explaining Philip Stanhope many years later to Mme. de Monconseil, was merely that the boy's mother 'had shown him favours he did not deserve.' But the Chesterfield of the Hague days had hardly reached his final view of what a great gentleman might or might not do. And, if Mlle. du Bouchet's case indeed demanded vengeance, her son certainly achieved it for her.

Chesterfield, at least, did thoroughly 'the right thing' by her, according to the standards of the time. On his resignation (for reasons of 'health and urgent private affairs') he brought her over to London, though his finances were in a desperate state, maintained her for the rest of her life, and gave little Philip his name and rather more than an ordinary father's care.

The 'Man of the World' now found himself in a dilemma. He had established a great reputation and, in doing so, had parted with the means to keep that reputation up. One cannot be a fine gentleman on a vanishing income. He sat down to review the matter calmly. It had become necessary to subordinate for the moment the minuet of fine living to the business of providing the means without which that or any other sort of living is impossible. 'I concluded,' he wrote frankly to the Earl of Essex, 'that it was high time to lay aside the fine gentleman and think of repairing my fortunes.'

To Baron Torck, a boon companion of the Hague, he was even more explicit. The Baron had been in precisely the same position, and had just found his way out of it. Chesterfield wrote to congratulate him; his is a really 'solid' marriage, he tells him; if there can be such a thing as a good marriage, this is it; for there is money, and the young woman is one who is least likely to irritate her husband. It is only right that marriage should pay for past pleasures, for it scarcely provides them for the future. He himself is not yet provided for; but La Bouchet will make no trouble – she knows there is no other way of supporting herself and her son. But he finds choice difficult, for he must have both merit and money; and the lady, on her side, must be one who is prepared to give much and receive little – to adapt herself to a wrecked constitution and repair wrecked affairs; he fears that this will prove to be La Fontaine's woman, who never was, nor will be.

She was found, however; but, again, not without payment. She was the Countess of Walsingham, a natural daughter of George I by Melusine of Schulenberg, who was politely known as her aunt. It was very definitely a French marriage *de convenance*. One of Chesterfield's letters to Baron Torck describing his hunt for a rich wife is dated January 1733, while that of October in the same year states that he has found her and is living the regular domestic life of a model husband – a fact which seems to dispose of the allusion to a long wooing by Maty, Chesterfield's official biographer, who wrote under his widow's direction. It is a pathetic little deception, and almost the only indication of the Countess's sentiments in the matter.

There was, however, a serious catch in the affair. George I had been fond of his daughter and had left her a large fortune, in addition to what she already had. But George II had quietly pocketed the will and it had never been seen since. It was reported, however, that another copy was in existence, safely in foreign hands. Chesterfield meant to have the full price of his liberty. He brought up the old scandal, and began to take legal steps. The King was practically blackmailed into a compromise, highly lucrative for Chesterfield and his wife; and George II, who had been somewhat conciliated by his conduct at the Hague, became Chesterfield's inveterate and permanent enemy.

There was no veil of politeness or diplomacy over George II's enmity. He sent the Duke of Grafton to demand the surrender of Chesterfield's white staff as Lord Steward of the Household. His Lordship, says Maty, cheerfully complied, and, without attempting any apology for his conduct, begged of his Grace to assure his Majesty that he was ready to sacrifice everything for his service except his honour and conscience. Whatever the German boor might do, Chesterfield would behave correctly. He attended the court at the first opportunity afterwards, but was so coldly received that he did not go again for many years. Henceforth his politeness to his sovereign was of the quality of King Hildebrand's:—

> *Go you and inform the lady,*
> *Most politely, most politely,*
> *If she don't, we'll storm the lady,*
> *Most politely, most politely.*

Chesterfield's political chances were ruined. He had now got back the means, and had lost the opportunity once more. On the other hand, he was never again crippled for want of money – that hopeless handicap to the rôle of fine gentleman. He had the large fortune that was his indispensable background.

Since he was once again inevitably in opposition, he took up his stand with a dramatic grace. In August 1733 he thanks the Countess of Suffolk (the former Mrs. Howard), for writing to him – 'A most uncommon piece of friendship and intrepidity,' since he is now called 'the King's enemy.' Besides, did she consider that her letter would probably be seen by Lovel and Carteret (the Postmasters-General) who will send it on to others 'of not inferior abilities and known dabs at finding out mysteries?' This distrust of the secrecy of the post appears in much of the correspondence of prominent men of the time, and Chesterfield made amusing use of this method of letting his opponents know what he thought of them. When he had any real plotting to do, he used a special courier. But he had no objection to referring to himself in this semi-publicity as a 'disgraced courtier.' Like all good actors, he carried his gestures through. If he could not be a successful courtier, he would be a very definite rebel.

Actually, with amazing persistence, he began to build again. The rule still held – one could not please one member of the House of Hanover without displeasing another, but the converse also was true, one could not displease one without pleasing another. George II's son was now to George II what he had been to George I. Again, Chesterfield had his chance of getting in with the heir, since he could not with the incumbent.

The opposition against Walpole and the Queen was

becoming by this time exceedingly lively and vocal. Walpole had been in office for fourteen years, a sufficient reason in itself. However well a statesman may acquit himself, grievances accumulate in a period of that length; other politicians are impatient for their turn; the public begins to feel that a change would be amusing. Walpole had done excellently for his country. He had saved it in an economic crisis; had put its finances on a sound basis and, against all probability, had kept the peace. England had had all the advantages of a dictatorship under a really first-rate dictator. Meanwhile, he maintained his position by a thoroughly organised system of corruption. He was nothing of a gentleman, and yet he got on well with everybody. Especially, he was on the best of terms with the Queen, the forceful personage who had thwarted Chesterfield's career from the outset. And he worked well with his colleagues. He had a coarse good-humour, a cajoling common-sense, so that it was almost impossible to have a personal quarrel with him; and he never bore a grudge.

On the other side were all the more picturesque elements of society, grouping themselves around Prince Frederick, who took the line of being very English indeed, and also, in rather awkward combination, a patron of arts and letters. The wits lampooned Walpole; journalists, poets, dramatists amused themselves at his expense. Chesterfield took his place in the circle with a flourish. In the House of Lords, he performed an elegant rapier dance around the King and his ministers, flicking, goading, withdrawing, bringing to such perfection the art of displeasing, that one wonders he did not undeceive himself as to the real nature of his genius. He will not allow the King power to deprive officers of their commissions without a court-martial – this is no attack on the prerogative, but merely a loyal desire that his Majesty should have the best information on which to act. Pensioners should not be allowed to sit in Parliament; naturally, if there is corruption, His Majesty can know nothing of it, but there may be others less innocent. Again, there are excellent state reasons why His Majesty should be deferentially requested to restrain his affection for his native Hanover.

At last, the theatres got completely out of hand, and lampooned Walpole scurrilously in a play called 'The Golden Rump.' Licensing restrictions were introduced hastily. Chesterfield produced a speech on the freedom of the press and the drama, which, in its lighter vein, might stand without disgrace beside the 'Areopagitica.' 'Wit is a property,' he points out, 'and too often, alas! the only property that those who have it have to depend on. We, thank God, my Lords! have a dependence of another kind' . . . 'I plead the cause of wit; I plead the cause of genius; and of every gentleman of taste in the Kingdom' – and, incidentally, the right to say what one chose of Robert Walpole. Walpole, however, as usual, put his measure through. A dumb, solid phalanx of bought voters cancelled wit, subtlety, logic, persistence. Chesterfield obtained debates, delays, caused sensations; he never won a motion. His success remained aesthetic.

It was, nevertheless, Chesterfield's heyday. He was a great figure – the Prince's chief courtier, his mentor and his model. The opposition court had a brilliant session at Bath in 1738, celebrating the birth of the Prince's son. Chesterfield did the honours. Beau Nash directed ceremonies. The eyes and the admiration of society were on him and his allies. Walpole, however, remained where he was. Even the Queen's death made no difference.

In every other sphere, than that which he had set his heart upon conquering, the great gentleman swept magnificently on his way. There were no more money troubles for him. He organised his ménage on lines that would have been advanced even in Paris. His wife continued to live with her mother next door to him in Grosvenor Square. He was always very polite to her, and never allowed her to interfere with his movements. A mercenary marriage can hardly by any standard be regarded as a graceful action, but it may be a rational bargain, which can be carried out with tact and courtesy. Chesterfield evidently regarded it in that light. Unfortunately, there is no issue about which ideas as to what constitutes tact and courtesy differ more than about that of matrimonial relations. The year after his marriage, Chesterfield's famous flirtation with Lady Fanny Shirley, the 'cold beauty,' was in full blossom – so discreetly, however, that no one ever knew for certain whether it was platonic or not. He had had the satisfaction of taking her from that same Lovel who probably read his letters.

> *Says Lovel, there were Chesterfield and Fanny,*
> *In that eternal whisper that begun*
> *Ten years ago and never will be done.*

'She is quit lost to me,' poor Lovel wrote. 'that foul fiend Chesterfield has bewitch't her, and, under pretence of serving me, has intirely defeated me and is in full possession of the Lady's soul; as for her body, that is so glorified that I presume none of our grosser mortal substance can ever think of that.'

Lovel, also, appears to have had some tincture of civilisation, for he gallantly played the buffoon over his misfortune. He revelled almost like a Boswell, in that humorous self-exposure which seemed ridiculous stupidity to the Victorian age, as it reacted towards reticence; but which is now again perfectly correct.

'I hear of nothing from London,' he laments, 'but his success all summer, partly by water, rides in Bushey Park, etc., and old Bitches begin to be censorious.' The difficulty of the lovers is that Chesterfield has to stand in his stirrups and Fanny to stoop to hear him; but Lovel is going to put that right by buying him a 'monstrous tall horse.'

One might, with a slight effort of imagination, make a romance out of this amour that lasted so long and inspired in Chesterfield the only one of his poems that has any verve, 'When Fanny, blooming fair,' (though even of that his authorship is disputed). In 1744, the old Duchess of Marlborough (Queen Anne's favourite), unexpectedly left Chesterfield, who had been polite and friendly to her in her forlorn old age, £20,000 and the reversion of her Wimbledon estate. If the legacy had come ten years earlier, perhaps his marriage would have been unnecessary and he would have been free for his Fanny. To add to the sentimental value of the situation, Fanny remained single to her death in 1778, at the age of seventy-two. Unfortunately, her last recorded words (Horace Walpole is, of course, the reporter) were not the name of her lover, but 'I to be abandoned whom all the world used to adore !' Nor did Chesterfield's own remarks on women and matrimony ever show much softening of the views expressed to Baron Torck. One suspects that the 'ten years' whisper' was merely a piquant minuet against the background of his colourless marriage.

But again, it is difficult to please everyone. There were even people uncivilised enough to disapprove of Chesterfield's treatment of his wife, who, though she appears to have been a silent, unobtrusive person, was occasionally indiscreet enough to let it appear (in confidence with her friends) that she did not enjoy her position as she should. When Chesterfield left the bulk of his money to his heir, and a comparatively small annuity to his wife, there was an outburst of bitter criticism ranging over his whole married life.

In the political sphere also, he had soon reason to know himself still unloved even by his 'friends.' Walpole fell at last in 1742. It had taken War, and War fever to bring him down, uttering his famous prophecy, 'Now they are ringing their bells; soon they will be wringing their hands.' Chesterfield's allies swarmed into office. It was a surprise to the public that Chesterfield was not among them. His private correspondence speaks gravely of honour and conscience. Rumour has given him position, he says, 'but I have been offered none, I have asked for none and I will accept of none till I see a little further into matters than I do at present.' Maty takes the occasion to deprecate some of the expressions that Chesterfield had used about his sovereign 'in the heat of debate.' Chesterfield carried off the victory and the set-back as he had carried off all the others. He did not speak on the vote of censure on Walpole, though he supported it, and he congratulated him when he entered the House of Lords. Horace Walpole describes a 'long laughing conversation' between the two ex-enemies at the King's levee. If Chesterfield supported the bill licensing government officials to give evidence against Walpole, it was evidently for some such reason as responsible statesmen supported the outcry to 'hang the Kaiser' in 1918. 'A free people,' he told the House of Lords, 'must be treated like a fine woman. If she has now and then a little caprice, you must not flatly contradict her. You must give way, or at least seem to give way, to her humour; till, by good treatment and a delicate opposition, you find an opportunity to give a turn to her temper.' The attitude justified itself. The clamour against Walpole died down, especially as the War soon turned out something less than a procession of triumphs.

For once, circumstances helped Chesterfield. The War went badly; and being 'still in opposition,' he was able to criticise it. The rôle suited him better than that of jingo. He was not a pacifist, but he was a diplomat, and had been out of his sphere as an advocate of War. He now found a happy compromise between the old and new attitude in insisting that England's part of the fighting should be confined to the sea, and Hanover's interests should be ignored. He was strong enough to force a fresh political crisis in 1744, and, at last, after ten years opposition, at the age of fifty, he was in office again. And, once again it was an office that took him out of the way. After a special embassy to the Hague, he was appointed Lord Lieutenant of Ireland. The King received him before his departure, in an audience that lasted forty-five seconds, and consisted in a single speech on His Majesty's side, 'You have your instructions, my Lord.'

The story of the Irish governorship is the story of the Hague ambassadorship again. Chesterfield did excellent work in this small sphere where he was absolute master; and he gave the government no peace until he was recalled. At his little court in Dublin, he was the biggest man in sight, and he treated his subjects and subordinates perfectly. His term of office – hardly more than a year – became a brief golden age in the Irish imagination. Throughout the crisis of the '45, when Ireland was expected to rise for the Pretender, he kept the peace not by repression, but by rational conciliation. He interviewed the most prominent Catholic in Dublin and promised him that if he would keep his friends quiet, there should be no persecution. He refused to burden the country by raising an army, and, when he was told by a scare-monger that the people of Connaught were rising, said that he believed it, since it was already nine o'clock. He was accessible to everyone. He refrained from gaming. He obtained a royal grant for the Dublin Society, which saw, as he did, that what Ireland needed was greater prosperity and not new political measures. In short, he gave Ireland a glimpse of true civilisation.

There, too, he enjoyed again the pleasures of patronage. He adds to his usual casual reason for 'choosing' Ireland – that there was 'enough business to prevent him from falling asleep and not so much as to keep him awake' – that he was now in a position to do something for people who had claims on him. In face of the King's opposition, his friend Chevenix was made Bishop of Waterford. Dayrolles, his protégé, became his Black Rod and afterwards Resident at the Hague.

A year later, he had won his point and his long delayed opportunity in English politics. Newcastle, the new comic opera prime-minister, who combined a sticking power almost equal to Walpole's with a farcical incompetence, made him joint Secretary of State with himself.

The arrangement lasted two years. By that time, Newcastle had worn out Chesterfield's patience, 'as indeed he has most people's.' The War was still going badly and Chesterfield wanted it ended, as did the French on their side. But the King and his ministers still hankered for spectacular military success. By September of 1747, Chesterfield was beginning to talk again of his preference for private life. 'It is disagreeable to tug at the oars with one who cannot row.' By January 1748, he will no longer be responsible for a policy he does not approve of and will no longer work in a position where he is well known to be a *commis* and 'has not been able to do a service to one man, though ever so meritorious.'

It was a reason too many. That Newcastle was a fool is admitted historical fact; but it seems equally clear that the man who made a fine art of pleasing could not have rowed long in the same boat with anyone at all. During a political life of over thirty years, he had failed to work peaceably with any colleague or superior. His successes were all made in situations where he was in undisputed control. Yet the slow, unwilling recognition that there is, after all, some fundamental incompatibility between the desire to shine and the desire to please came to him only in his old age.

Chesterfield's political career ended at fifty-four with his resignation from Newcastle's ministry. He never tried again; but fell back into *otium cum dignitate* – a favourite phrase of his for that resting upon his laurels which seemed to him correct for the great gentleman, already becoming elderly and in failing health, who has shaken the dust of politics off his feet. 'From politics he rather escaped well than succeeded by them,' was Horace Walpole's verdict. And that he should have seemed even to escape well is a tribute to Chesterfield's technique. A man who cannot control his tongue has little chance in politics. George II might at last perhaps have forgiven the raid upon his pocket; but it was not in human nature to forgive the man who had allowed himself to say, 'If we have a mind effectually to prevent the Pretender from ever obtaining the crown, we should make him Elector of Hanover, for the people of England will never fetch another King from thence.' But even when George II had been overborne, Chesterfield's political career lasted just three years.

Otium cum dignitate, even with a flavour of sour

grapes, seems, in fact, a sound ideal for the declining years of a fine gentleman. The quieter social pleasures, cultured leisure, patronage of the arts, the polishing of promising youth, the obligations of a large fortune and high rank to friends and dependents, this was surely a wide enough sphere, and Chesterfield turned hopefully to it. There was a bout of gambling at White's just after his resignation – as both Maty and Horace Walpole, friend and enemy, remark on it, it must have been something quite conspicuous. Then it was time for more placid pursuits. Chesterfield set about building the fine town house that bore his name, and to filling it with pictures and objects of *vertu* for which his correspondents ransacked Europe; he cultivated melons at his country house at Blackheath; he helped poets and authors; he kept open house in London and in Bath during the season, and even at fifty-eight created a pretty little scandal with Princess ——; he kept up an enormous and varied correspondence; he contributed light, elegant essays to the *World*. He had the Calendar corrected by Parliament in spite of Newcastle's Gilbertian pleading 'not to stir matters that had long been quiet'; and the brilliant success of his speech on this occasion, compared with Lord Macclesfield's solid, scientific contribution, 'worth a thousand of mine,' formed the text of a sermon to young Stanhope on the uselessness of 'matter' without 'manner.'

And here was a more poignant interest. Young Stanhope, the son of Mlle. du Bouchet, was now sixteen and had received a most careful and solid education. He had started on the Grand Tour with his tutor with the object of adding the graces to his equipment and of becoming a perfect man of the world. Chesterfield concentrated on his development with the desperation of a man who finds himself, after all, obliged to leave much of the accomplishment he had hoped for to the next generation. His marriage had brought him no children. Young Stanhope could not be his heir, but he was the sole continuator of his existence. Even before Chesterfield's retirement, the boy's training had become a burning question to him. During his busiest years as Lord-Lieutenant of Ireland and as Secretary of State, he had bombarded with didactic letters this young hobbledehoy who, it seemed, could learn everything except to behave gracefully in society. And other letters, to the Marquise de Monconseil in Paris, almost burst the shell of polite compliment, begging, exhorting, adjuring her to polish for him this rough diamond, of whom he says, in a passage of surprising vehemence written in the critical year of the '45, 'my affection, or, if you will, my weakness for this boy makes all that happens to him infinitely more poignant than anything that could happen to myself.'

It is, in fact, the one authentic note of passion to be found in any manifestation of Chesterfield's personality that remains; and it is found rather in the letters written about Philip than in those written to him. It was an unusual type of passion. It appears, indeed, to have been that 'desire for his perfection' which Plato describes as the highest kind of love. Unfortunately, it is not the kind that is apt to bring the readiest response. Philip Stanhope seems to have been as bored and embarrassed by it as most young people are by their parents' efforts to form their characters. And perhaps his intuition was sound.

'Why do you think I have this affair so extremely at heart? And why do I repeat it so often? Is it for your sake or for mine?' the father demands in desperation. It was intended to be a rhetorical question; but it is a pertinent one. Chesterfield had tried in his own life to create the perfect man, as he saw that elusive ideal. But one life had not proved long enough. He longed to pass on his acquired experience to those who still had time to use it; it was poured out on every youngster with whom he came in contact, from Prince Frederick and young Lord Huntingdon, to the younger Philip Stanhope, his heir, with even a crumb or two thrown to the latter's bright little sister. But this older Philip Stanhope was a creature utterly at his disposal. His illegitimacy made his dependence complete, and, when pressed sufficiently hard, Chesterfield did not scruple to use it against him. 'I do not so much as hint to you,' he says, 'how absolutely dependent you are upon me, that you neither have, nor can have, a shilling in the world except from me.' Philip was fourteen when this hint was so carefully not given. Chesterfield saw him as so much raw material out of which he would yet fashion the perfect 'Man of the World.' 'I admit,' he tells Mme. de Monconseil, just before the crucial year in Paris which was to be the coping-stone of Philip's education, 'I am impatient, like an author, to see a fine and correct edition of my work.'

He could not see why it could not be done. It was again that eighteenth century rationality, which sometimes, paradoxically, seems to us, inured by modern psychology to the emotional complexity of human nature, to be pathetically childish. He could not see why young people could not learn from the experience of their elders, and carry on from where they left off. It was just for want of such a guide, he tells Philip, that he himself sometimes took the wrong path. If anyone had taken such pains with him, he would have avoided many follies; but his own father had been neither willing nor able to advise him. One speculates what might have happened if

Chesterfield's father had indeed been a man of strong character with an impulse to form the young. It seems unlikely that his ideal would have coincided with that which seemed to Chesterfield the only one possible for a rational man.

Friends protested against the incessant moral manhandling of young Philip. Lady Hervey, Chesterfield tells the boy frankly, blames him for trying to make him perfect. He has a good head, she points out, a good heart, a good fund of knowledge, why worry about more? He is loved wherever he is known. But Chesterfield will have him liked *before* he is known. Mme. de Monconseil, Chesterfield's crony of the salons, seems to have been almost superhumanly patient and hopeful with this unpromising lump of raw material. But even she drops a hint that Chesterfield perhaps attaches too much importance to the bark of the tree. It isn't, Chesterfield assures her in reply, that he prefers frivolous graces to solid worth – for why is it necessary to choose between them? 'I will absolutely that our boy have them; I threaten, I flatter, I fulminate in turn.' He is having Philip home for an overhaul in August (Philip was then eighteen), but will send him back to her afterwards. In chronic evils, remedies must be persistent. If he is clumsy when Chesterfield meets him, he will have a fever. He cannot endure it even in people he cares nothing about.

Did it ever occur to Chesterfield that his methods might be mistaken? There are spasmodic attempts at another mode of treatment in the letters. He claims a position of friendship rather than of authority. 'The authority of a parent shall be for ever laid aside,' he promised in 1749, 'for wherever it is exerted, it is useless; since if you have neither sense nor sentiments enough to follow my advice as a friend, your unwilling obedience to my orders as a father, will be very awkward and unavailing both to yourself and to me.' When Philip is seventeen, the letters cease to open 'Dear boy' and begin henceforward 'My dear friend.' After another plea for intimate friendship, follows the passage, 'Your letters except when upon a given subject are exceedingly laconic and neither answer my desires, nor the purpose of letters.' He recommends a study of Mme. de Sévigné's letters in order to learn the fluent intimacy which is proper in such a relation.

One can imagine Philip's comments to his companions in those continental cities which he paraded so long in search of *les manières nobles*. He had to be very careful. Everywhere, Chesterfield had watchful correspondents – he did not hide the fact from Philip. They were always sending him reports. Everywhere, there were introductions to be followed up, and accounts of the results would be demanded. Money for 'refined pleasures' was absolutely unstinted. 'As to the expense which you mention I do not regard it in the least. . . . I bar no expense that has neither vice nor folly for its object. . . . Draw and welcome.'

But if any money goes on low pleasures he will soon know of it.

No independent witness, and (after the posthumous publication of the letters) there were many, suggests that Philip Stanhope was a bad sort of youth. The things he could learn, he learnt. He was erudite, and even developed a taste for old editions. He acquired all the useful modern languages; he had a good business head and did his job well enough when he got one. He may even have tried to please; but he was badgered, spied upon, given away, forced upon people whom he did not want and who did not want him. Mme. de Monconseil is told to take an authoritative tone with him, laugh at him, make him ridiculous, if necessary, let him off nothing. Let him be her page, let her treat him anyway she likes. Lord Huntingdon is adjured to 'look upon him as your dependent, your client, your creature.' And Philip himself is given corresponding instructions. Even his love-affairs are supervised. There is Mme. de Blot, his father tells him, a beautiful young woman of fashion, who has gauchely remained faithful to her husband, although they have been married a year. Why shouldn't she and Philip *décrotter* each other? Then there is Mme. Dupin, who would not be incompatible with the other. She has still enough beauty for *un jeune drôle comme vous* (these passages are always in French) and she has wit and refinement and not too much choice now. When the letters came to be published, the moral tone of such exhortations shocked even the most favourable of Chesterfield's critics, who did not recognise in them the driving force of a quite ruthless, though alien, morality.

Even a lad of natural good manners might well have become defensive under such treatment. Philip's were not naturally good. It must have been on that occasion of the 'overhauling' that the incident of the gooseberries and the cream occurred, described with so much gusto by Lord Charlemont. Seeing the entrancing dish about to be carried away, young Philip hastily recalled it and plunged into it with such abandon that his father turned to the servant, 'John, why do you not fetch the strop and the razors? You see your master is going to shave himself.'

'I will never,' had optimistically promised the Chesterfield of the Letters, 'put you out of countenance before company.' But the undertaking proved to be beyond his strength.

This was the youth to whom for years past he had been pouring out advice on the more subtle points of social behaviour – how to bear himself to friends, opponents, superiors, equals, inferiors, how to manage women by flattery and men through their ruling passions, how to take jokes and ward off disputes, how to guide the conversation without appearing to do so, how to treat the Jacobites when he met them, to avoid laughter and anecdote, to practise the art of engaging badinage; in short, to have 'a distinguished politeness, an almost irresistible address; a superior gracefulness in all you say and do.' Other defects than blatant greed also appeared in young Philip. He had an absent and supercilious air, a sullen expression, a scholar's stoop, a bad enunciation – in fact, all that could most offend his father's taste, and all that might be expected of a boy whose self-consciousness had been stimulated by every possible means throughout his adolescence.

About 1752, Chesterfield began to give Philip up. He is going to Germany, he tells Mme. de Monconseil, and not likely to get there the coats of varnish that even Paris could not give him. It was a bad year for Chesterfield. Hereditary deafness was coming upon him, perhaps the worst infliction from which a man of society could suffer. His general health had been poor for many years and to real intimates he often wrote of himself in the late fifties, as of an old man with one foot in the grave – perhaps happily unaware of the twenty years still before him. The passion of a Pygmalion gradually dies out of his letters to and about Philip; and, as it does so, they take on a certain charm. For this relationship of father to son was, after all, a human relationship to be conducted gracefully; and, if Chesterfield had often forgotten this aspect of the matter in his desperate efforts to make his son the sequel to himself, he now remembered it again. He did not allow his disappointment to betray him into any ugly action. Several times he had threatened to withdraw his support, if Philip ever showed that he did not deserve it. And, from his father's point of view, he did not deserve it. But his father nevertheless continued to push his fortunes with the utmost solicitude. He bought him a seat in Parliament (it was not necessary for Philip to return to England in order to stand for it) and wrote him a consoling letter when he broke down in his maiden speech. He gave him an introduction to Voltaire – at that time, from some points of view, the highest favour that could be done to a young man. At Hanover, in 1752, came Philip's crucial presentation to the King. It seemed a remarkable audacity to expect George II to stretch a point for the illegitimate son of the man who had married his own illegitimate sister at his expense, and Chesterfield was obviously nervous about it; but Stanhope was received, though coldly. He had more success with the amiable idiot, Newcastle, and there was talk of his appointment as Resident at Venice. 'If the thing succeeds,' wrote Chesterfield, who had once spoken of Philip as a future Secretary of State, 'it will make me happier than, in my present situation, any one thing in the world could make me.' But the sins of the father fell upon the son, and George II blocked the young man's advancement. Soon afterwards young Stanhope had to be hurriedly smuggled from Brussels, where the presentation of a bastard to the Emperor's brother had got Dayrolles into trouble.

Philip did nothing to help himself. There was a final outburst from Chesterfield in a letter to Mme. de Monconseil. Philip has spent seven years in all the countries of Europe, meeting all the best people. He ought to be a master in the art of pleasing, whereas he is still a long way even from the bare necessities. How can he have a good mind, and docility, as she says he has, and not recognise the necessity for pleasing? If he isn't convinced of the necessity now, when will he be? A thousand persons have said all they could to him on the subject, and Chesterfield himself has dealt with it exhaustively by letter, making clear a self-evident proposition. A little of the writer's exasperation seems almost to overflow upon the poor lady herself.

Young Stanhope was ultimately pushed into diplomacy through an inferior post at Hamburgh, and held such posts creditably until his early death in 1768. After his death, appeared Mrs. Eugenie Stanhope, another gentleman's bastard of a suburban gentility, whose acquaintance Philip had made in Rome during his Grand Tour, and who had been with him at Hamburgh for many years. There is no indication whether her existence and that of her two small sons was really the shock to Chesterfield that it was popularly supposed to be. A letter to Stanhope at Hamburgh in 1759 begs him to give details of his domestic life, adding significantly, 'whenever you condescend to do it, stick to truth, for I am not so ill-informed of Hamburgh as perhaps you may think.' But the young man had now the advantage, and Chesterfield recognised it with a good grace. A few months later he says that he will not ask again, 'you have sworn not to tell me.' And the letters, now about political and diplomatic affairs, town gossip, extra allowances for Philip, with very few allusions to 'les graces,' continued. 'I never receive a letter of yours,' Chesterfield wrote, 'but I answer it by the next post, or the next but one, at furthest.'

Whether Mrs. Eugenie was a shock to him or not,

Chesterfield treated her perfectly. He wrote her friendly letters, and supported and educated her boys. A playful letter to them, with hardly a flavour of instruction, was one of his last.

Arising out of the ideals of decency, good taste, 'les manières nobles,' the later Chesterfield seems indeed to have developed a sense of obligation that had almost the binding force of Roman 'piety.' He had been a careless son, a light lover, a disloyal husband. He had no family pride – among his portraits were two labelled 'Adam de Stanhope' and 'Eve de Stanhope.' Philip Stanhope the younger, his heir, had it drummed into him that the great position he was to inherit was accidental and had no connection with personal merit. Nevertheless, Chesterfield's attitude to his friends, his friend's friends, anyone who had ever worked for him or had any shadow of claim on him, had become almost feudal. Many of his letters are concerned with asking, granting or advising about the advancement of such protégés. He offers tactfully to pay the debts of the younger Dayrolles even before he has mentioned that he has any. Anyone who ever asked Chesterfield for advice seems to have received not mere superficial suggestions, but a carefully thought-out analysis of the situation and the various courses open, with offers of help, whenever possible.

It was just here, where the great gentleman seemed least vulnerable, that chance played her worst trick upon him. Many poets and literary men whose names are forgotten had been helped by him. The greatest literary personality of the age conceived himself slighted by him and used his command of language to write him a masterpiece of polite insult, such as Chesterfield himself never attained to, and so powerful that for nearly two centuries it has shown the man to whom courtesy was the highest duty as the most overbearing and neglectful.

'Seven years, my Lord, have now passed since I waited in your outward rooms, and was repulsed from your door, during which I have been pushing on my work through difficulties of which it is useless to complain and have brought it, at last, to the verge of publication, without one act of assistance, one word of encouragement, or one smile of favour.'

The probable facts have long been admitted. Johnson's own strong conscience drove him later to attach to a copy of the famous letter a statement that he had, in fact, received a subscription of £10 from Chesterfield, 'but as that was so inconsiderable a sum, he thought the mention of it could not properly find place in a letter of the kind that this was.' Certainly, one should not spoil a poem for £10, or even, perhaps, for someone's reputation. As to the repulse, it appears that Johnson was once kept waiting a short time while Chesterfield (then Secretary of State) interviewed a poet whom Johnson justifiably considered very much his inferior.

The psychological truth of the situation is not difficult to guess at. It was a question, on the one side, of an over-sensitive man of genius, taught by painful experience to be on the watch for slights, and who needed something more than formal courtesy – sympathy, insight that would recognise the power of which he alone could then be conscious, the kind of help that ideally a man in Chesterfield's position could most ideally give. On the other side, was a busy man of affairs, anxious to be every-one's friend, but, for that very reason, with very little time for any one individual, and no special gift for divining hidden fire. But the letter is absolute; it was so good that it had to be true. No lover of literature could endure that it should not be.

There is, after all, a certain crude justice in the episode. Chesterfield was trying to be superhuman; he was trying to regulate all human relationships by a superfine rationality. In the parable of Chesterfield's career, Johnson was the symbol of the essential unreasonableness of life that the other always refused to accept.

That Chesterfield recognised the beauties of the great letter almost redeems him – for eternity, if not for time. He kept it and showed it to his friends, remarking on the great powers of its writer and pointing out the best passages – a display of civilised detachment, comparable to Clive Bell's example of the Athenians, besieged and in the acme of war fever, giving a public performance to a satire on militarism and patriotism. In fact, Chesterfield did rather more, he bestowed on the letter the highest form of flattery. 'Neither pride or modesty,' Johnson had written, 'would suffer me to continue it.' In a letter written about the same time, Chesterfield declines an invitation. 'Both my pride and my modesty,' he says, 'forbid me to exhibit my *chétive figure* in good company.'

Reasoned courtesy does not perhaps foster that delicacy of perception which would have enabled the courtesy to be applied to the best advantage. The same insensitiveness which lost Chesterfield Johnson's powerful advocacy – that enabled him to use his son's illegitimacy against him, and to approach Queen Caroline through her husband's mistress – appears many times in his career. Sometimes it seems to be allied to that other characteristic of civilised man – determined realism, the urge to see things as they are and to say so, together with a frequently unwarranted expectation that other people will do likewise. There is an odd letter to the younger Dayrolles on the death of his uncle, who had also been Chesterfield's friend and protégé; –

'I make you no compliments of condolence upon the death of your uncle, for, though I loved him very well, I love you better and you are now easy and independent.' Dayrolles was in no position to resent this, even if he wished to do so. Nor was ten-year-old Philip Stanhope, the younger, when Chesterfield, even in his mellowing old age, wrote reassuringly to him that, if his father was imprudent enough to marry again, especially a young girl, he would see that he did not lose by it, but perhaps gain. He adds carefully that he does not know for certain that this is going to happen, but he suspects it, since people who marry twice will marry twenty times if they live long enough, 'and much good may it do them.' Philip's father had, in fact, already consulted Chesterfield on the subject and received a characteristic reply. Chesterfield never gives advice on religion and matrimony 'because he will not have anyone's torment in this world or the next laid to his charge.' He then proceeds to give it. No doubt, he (Mr. Stanhope) is lonely and melancholy, but loneliness is better than bad company, which a wife would probably be. Chesterfield has sincerely never thought a woman good company for a man, tête-à-tête, unless for one purpose, which presumably does not apply in this case. Mr. Stanhope already has two fine children, what should he want with more? He is in no position to provide for them. Chesterfield's own brother gave just the same reasons for marrying and said he had found a retiring, domesticated young woman; and the outcome is notorious.

Needless to say, Mr. Stanhope married, though, on all other matters, his deference to the Head of the Family is almost painful.

Against little Philip, who had succeeded the elder one as the heir presumptive of Chesterfield's personality as well as of his title and estates, the cleverness of his young sister is used, in a manner to make boil the blood of a modern child-lover. The two children were very fond of each other, but the girl was the superior in quickness and application. No opportunity was lost to rub this in to Philip and presently Chesterfield announced triumphantly to the boy's father that he had become 'horribly jealous of her.' 'It is right,' he adds, 'that these little fears and jealousies should be kept alive.'

And yet, in spite of these spiritual crudities, there is a difference in tone in the later correspondence with the little Philip. In 1762, at the age of six, he is given rules for the behaviour of a well-bred gentleman. Three years later, begin a series on the Art of Pleasing. The same old maxims are repeated. But there is now less emphasis on the necessity of pleasing people for what one may get out of them, more on the desirability of satisfactory human relationships in themselves. Little Philip's duty to man is 'only to do unto others as you would they should do to you. This duty extends to politeness, gentleness and manners; for you surely wish that everyone should show them towards you, so show them to everyone.' Chesterfield works out the philosophy of it in terms that must have been above the head of the child. We are all individually helpless and dependent on each other, he points out. No one can get food, clothes, beds or shelter by himself. One must therefore repay by help, indulgence, charity, 'loving people' which is called 'philanthropy.' Christianity adds that we should love even our enemies. But 'as love and hate is not in our power, though our actions are, this commandment means no more than that instead of resenting or revenging injuries we should return good for evil. For example, if my enemy were hungry, or naked, or in sickness, or in pain, I would relieve him to the utmost of my power; and so would you, I am sure, because you are a good-natured, benevolent boy.'

Philip must never neglect the common duties of social life. (He had not been writing regularly to his father.) Even amongst common acquaintances negligence is a kind of insult. . . . 'Whenever you are a little wanting in attention, let it be only to me, for I think you and I are so well together, that we shall reciprocally forgive little inadvertencies.'

There are many such charming little bids for the boy's friendship in these letters, as if Chesterfield had at least partly divined the stumbling-block in his treatment of the older Philip – that he had put 'passion for his perfection' before the establishment of a satisfactory relationship between himself and the boy in the first place. The younger Philip was being educated in London under Chesterfield's own eye and was often with him. But the frequent assurances to his father that he governs the child by love, not by fear, tell their story of misgiving. Philip, after all, found this deaf old man, who held him between his knees to insist on his attention, more formidable than attractive.

'I must observe,' wrote Chesterfield to Mr. Stanhope, 'that he can disguise himself wonderfully; for when he is with me, he is very grave and I can hardly prevail with him to be young; but upon enquiring ten days ago of Mr. Robert into his private character, he assured me that he was the noisiest, running, jumping, singing, dancing boy he ever saw and that a few more such would turn his head.' Nor did Philip ever show Chesterfield the gusts of temper of which other people complained. The old diplomat consoled himself that 'he ought to make an able minister.'

Chesterfield never lived to see how his second venture turned out. When he died, the boy was still away on the

Grand Tour. In later life, like the elder Philip, he held one or two minor appointments, and he was at court when Fanny Burney was Maid of Honour. She remarks devastatingly in her diary:—'Lords Chesterfield, Harrington and Cathcart drank tea with us almost constantly. The two latter I liked extremely.' And she describes elsewhere a tactless practical joke of Philip's, lamenting his lack of breeding.

The Man of the World, after all, left no one to carry on the torch, though he mercifully did not know it. It could not burn bright in the old man himself, who was a deaf invalid for the last twenty years of his life. He had been carried from the House of Lords in 1755, after a vigorous speech, and never spoke there again. His intercourse with people became more and more limited to correspondence. Already in 1753, he was writing to Mme. de Monconseil that he is now happier with distant friends; a friend in person overwhelms him and brings home his misfortune. He is vegetating, gardening, walking, reading – waiting for death without desiring or fearing it. 'I do not play the Stoic philosopher,' he says, 'I feel my ill and agree that it is such, but at the same time I feel by experience that one can have much more control of oneself than is generally supposed. I seek out everything that can amuse me, and make diversion of the gloomy reflections which my misfortune would otherwise inspire. I am ready for the least amusements, try to augment them and to make an object of them, so that, with the help of a naturally gay temperament, I am still secure from melancholy.' There was still a more dramatic gesture for the public ear. 'Lord—— and I have been dead these twelve years, but we do not wish it known.'

Voltaire wrote consolingly that a good digestion is worth a pair of ears – he himself is in a position to judge whether it is worse to be deaf, blind or digestionless – and added the spontaneous testimonial, 'You have never been in the class of charlatans, or dupes of charlatans.' There were honours from the French Academy, presents from the Czarina. Public feeling had softened towards Chesterfield, as always towards the old who have been famous figures. Enemies are disarmed when one is no longer dangerous. When he was over seventy, people still laughed before they knew what he had said, remarked Horace Walpole, adding unkindly that perhaps they would not if they waited to hear. But even Horace Walpole entertained the old man at Strawberry Hill in his later years and exchanged polite badinage with him.

It must, none the less, have been a weary stretch from 1755, when he was already expecting imminent death, to 1773. It is a severe test for a 'man of the world' to be old, ill, deaf and disappointed for some twenty years. Perhaps it was the greatest achievement of Chesterfield's life that he never became bad-tempered. 'His politeness,' said the doctor at his deathbed, 'deserts him only with his life.'

Only a religion can effect this kind of thing. Chesterfield's ideal of fine conduct had, in fact, developed into a religion. It consolidated with age and actually gained in strength when he had nothing more to expect or hope from other people. He approached that other definition of a 'Gentleman' as 'one who brushes his teeth just before he goes to the dentist.'

The later Chesterfield's spiritual home was further afield than the French salons and his ideal passed beyond that perfection of human nature – the cultured Frenchman. Only in the oldest civilisation of the East, is found that perfect code of human behaviour that would have given him peace of mind. Like him, the Confucians of China felt no need of any supernatural sanction. To know how to behave well in every conceivable situation was enough for them. Chesterfield, marooned in the wrong time and place, had to create himself in an intractable environment. Only once was Confucius disconcerted – when he met the saintly mystic, Lao-Tsze. And Lao-Tsze, on his side, was amused. They found nothing in common. If the later Chesterfield could have met the Christian mystic, St. Francis, perhaps that more human saint would also have been amused, but he would certainly have found some common ground. For courtesy, in its widest sense, can cover almost everything.

Chesterfield's last words were not a *bon mot*, but a simple request to give his visitor a chair.

In England, he became a legend, but never an ideal. His personal heirs failed him, and he had no spiritual heirs. Nothing, however, could well be further from the point than Horace Walpole's summing up: 'One perceives by what infinite assiduity and attention his Lordship's own great character was raised and supported, and yet in all that great character what was worth remembering, but his *bons mots*?' He left, in fact, the challenging phenomenon of a remarkable, if imperfect, work of art.

ACKNOWLEDGMENTS

In Section III the quotations from Lord Lovel's letters, on pages 111 and 112, first appeared in Roger Coxon's *Chesterfield and his Critics*, published by Routledge.

IV
THE CHILD OF NATURE

AMONG the various plans of living that have caught the imagination of mankind from time to time one that constantly recurs is that of the 'Simple Life.' It appears whenever civilisation has so far developed that it seems at last fairly safe from outside enemies. The builders of Jerusalem win sufficient respite to lay down their weapons for a moment and to look with a critical eye at what they have been building. Some of them are inevitably dissatisfied; a few are so disgusted that they are soon wondering whether it was worth doing at all, and whether they would not, after all, be happier without it. There follows a revulsion towards whatever, in the knowledge and speculation of the time, men suppose to be primitive simplicity. Aristocrats begin to play at being Arcadian shepherds and shepherdesses; authors choose for their heroes Indian chiefs or Arab sheiks; practical philosophers retire into the wilderness, or organise back-to-nature movements.

Such a phase arrived towards the end of the eighteenth century when civilisation was just preparing to turn furiously upon itself in the French Revolution. The 'natural man' ideal appeared as the inevitable foil of the Chesterfield ideal of a completely artificial code of behaviour.

Which of the two was, in fact, the more 'natural' may remain a debatable point; as Rousseau himself, the evangelist of the new gospel, remarked, 'much art is required to prevent man in society from being altogether artificial.' Moreover, Arab chiefs and Afghan kings, introduced to civilisation, do not always show the contempt which one might expect.

However, the eighteenth century, a little disgusted with its own sophistication, had looked round for something with which to compare itself to its disadvantage and had discovered the 'Noble Savage.' Essential beauty and virtue, since they were not in the present, must be in the past; they had belonged to man in his primitive conditions. Civilisation was a journey of exit from the Garden of Eden. It was, of course, greatly to the advantage of this theory that very little was actually known about primitive man. Out of the immense mass of systematised material now existing – comparative studies of savage customs, of folk-lore, of antiquities, minute scientific observation of living races – only scattered details were then available, such as could, at a pinch, be made to support any view. The searchlight of Evolution was not yet unveiled.

At this moment, the Ossian poems, faked ancient Gaelic epics, swept the country and the continent like a modern 'best-seller.' The heroes of Ossian were the Sir Charles Grandisons of the wilds – courteous, sensitive, gentle and magnanimous. They fought, but with all the conventions of chivalry. They let off defeated foes, they threw aside their armour to meet an enemy on equal terms; they were constantly dying for love; when they were not fighting or hunting, they were composing poetry. John Smith of Kilbranden, a minor 'collector' of Ossianic poems, gives an illuminating picture of the eighteenth century notion of primitive man. Conditions in ancient Caledonia, he suggests, must have been particularly favourable to moral virtue; there was plenty of room and plenty of game for everybody and therefore no occasion for jealousies; the Caledonians were therefore 'strong in their attachments and even violent in their friendships.' They were isolated from corrupting influences. 'It is only when society advances and the number and wants of men grow many, that their interests begin to jostle and interfere, so as to kindle and by their collision bring to light a thousand vices till then unknown.' He accepts the theory that the ancient Highlanders had only one meal a day, and considers that this abstinence 'had a benign aspect to every virtue, but was peculiarly favourable to that delicacy with which we find the tender sex always treated by Ossian's heroes.' Macpherson himself, the original forger of the Ossian epics, had already pointed out, with pardonable pride, Ossian's 'partiality to the fair sex,' in contrast with Homer's disdainful treatment of it; but had failed to note the doubtless relevant fact that Homer's heroes feast three times in one night.

This literary and aesthetic day-dream remained, of course, a day-dream for most people, though it had the perilous potentialities of such fantasies. Such things get into the atmosphere, modify thought and feeling insensibly, give a semblance of form to vague discontents. Moreover, the movement had its philosophers as well as its poets. Rousseau, one of the most dangerous men who ever lived (whether the word is used in a good, or a bad sense), had started the intellectual attack on modern civilisation with his heavy opening gun: 'Man is born free, and everywhere he is in chains'; and had never quite caught up his effect with the following demonstration that man, though born free, is also born helpless. It is one of the philosopher's risks that his followers will miss the balancing factors of which he himself may be well aware. Rousseau never tried to act out his theories. But other people did, and one man, an Englishman, Thomas Day, tried to live them completely.

Rousseau's closest effort to get down to brass tacks – to show the 'natural life' in working – was not in the *Social Contract*, which had such immense political effects, but in *Émile*, his plan for the education of youth.

Émile is the son of wealthy parents, 'for the poor man needs no education, since the conditions of his life force one upon him.' Therefore an entirely natural growth has to be insured for Émile by elaborately contrived circumstances. He is to live in the country, and mix in social equality with the peasants. He is to learn everything by direct investigation and experience, and the result of mistaken actions is to be his only punishment. If he yelled in the night as a child, his tutor would refuse to come near him. If he did not want to learn to read, there was some pleasant invitation which he would fail to accept because he could not read it. In fact, he was to correspond to a modern novelist's definition of an Aristocrat as one who 'does what he likes and takes the consequences.'

But, even if he learned to read, he would have little to do with books in his early childhood, and much with nature. Locke's principle of reasoning with children would never be applied to him; he would find out for himself. No religion would be imposed upon him; he would develop his own as he could.

Then, at a suitable age, he would be given *Robinson Crusoe*, and this would become his Bible. 'I would have his head turned with it,' said Rousseau. He would learn elementary economics in imitating Crusoe; would build his own shack, make his own clothes, kill his own game. Anything he could not provide for himself he would get with trouble and difficulty, learning in the process how it was made and at what expense of labour, and that it was necessary to have the goodwill of his fellows and to repay them in some way in order to obtain it. A little later, he must have a craft of his own, preferably carpentering, and would take an intelligent interest in other crafts. He would visit workshops and factories, where he would never see any labour without putting his own hand to the work, nor go away without perfectly knowing the reason of all that he had observed. At adolescence, which would probably be deferred by a life full of practical interest and activity, he would be introduced to literature and to society, as he showed himself ripe for them. 'Émile is not a savage to be banished to a desert, he is a savage made to live in towns. He must know how to find his subsistence there, to hold his own among their inhabitants, and to live, if not like them, at least, with them.' At last, he would be unobtrusively led into meeting a girl who had also been brought up on 'natural' lines, and the coping-stone would be put upon his education.

Émile's training was, in fact, to be guided less by Nature than by Necessity. He would be compelled to recognise those fundamental facts which are hidden from the town child, who is provided with the things it needs without knowing what they really are, or where they come from; and is taught to theorise out of books, before it has any chance to find out what the words in the books stand for. It is the difference between making a map by surveying a country, and copying it out of an atlas.

Unfortunately, the expense, devotion and ingenuity necessary in order to give young Émiles natural conditions in the midst of a highly developed society have always barred any such experiment on a large scale. The plain hard fact is that, in only one case in a million, if so many, would anyone be prepared to go to so much trouble over one child. Modern education has tried various approximations to it, which seem to have proved their value. There was one group of children, now grown-up, who came near to it by happy accident, and are now convinced that the best and most illuminating part of their education was an attempt to live the life of Red Indians according to Thompson Seton's *Two Little Savages*. This book 'turned their heads' as *Robinson Crusoe* turned Émile's. One wonders why it is not regarded as a children's classic on another and higher plane than the adult slynesses of *Alice in Wonderland* and *Peter Pan* – unless, indeed, parents have formed a conspiracy of silence about it. It tells one – with diagrams and minute directions – how to make bows and arrows, rubbing-stick fires, fur-bough beds, moccasins, war paint and a teepee to live in; how to build dams, to track animals and leave secret signals for fellow-tribesmen. It is a rule of the game that all this is to be done without civilised tools. Nothing is allowed but what Nature provides. There had to be concessions, of course, but they were given like drops of blood. One must have a knife and a hatchet, and unplaned arrows do not fly straight; but every such lapse is a mark against one, which is never forgotten. So far as in them lay, with all the handicap of the English climate and the inferior products of the English soil, the children followed their hero's gospel. Nothing would deter them. They nauseated their elders with 'cured' rabbit-skins, outraged their nerves with raids and war-dances, terrified them by sleeping out in a rickety teepee and by turning out in the night with axe and arrows to drive off a drunken tramp. And, over months, with blood and tears and rapture, they learned what life must have been like for primitive man. They were confronted, like him, with nothing but Nature and their bare hands. Food, clothes, houses, furniture, cars, trains, telephones, have never been to them matters to be taken for granted. It is not a bad prologue to a course of lectures at the School of Economics.

Two Little Savages would have delighted Rousseau. It was just this freshness of apprehension that he wanted for his ideal boy. And the fascination of Émile's personality was great to a generation discontented with civilised life, and accustomed to precocious, affected little ladies and gentlemen. Émile at fifteen was to be like this:—

'He considers himself without regard to others, and thinks it well that others are not thinking of him. He exacts nothing of anyone and believes that he owes nothing to anyone. He is alone in human society and counts only upon himself. He has also more right than others to count upon himself, for he is all that one can be at his age. He has no faults, or only those that are inevitable to us; he has no vices, or only those against which no man can insure himself. He has a sound body, agile limbs, a just and unprejudiced mind and a heart free and without passions.'

The dramatic possibilities of the impact of such a personality on Society delighted the eighteenth century. Émile was nearer to life than the Ossian heroes; he had a robustness, a humour, an insouciance that they had not. Novel after novel, beginning with Brooke's *Fool of Quality*, showed Émiles as *enfants terribles* devastating eighteenth century drawing-rooms.

To a modern mind, there seems to be no reason why 'Sophie,' the ideal girl and Émile's destined bride, should not have been brought up very much as he was. But Rousseau, original in most things, was normal in this – that he had more conventional ideals for the other sex than for his own. He conceived the 'nature' of women in quite other terms. It was to be 'He for Nature only, she for Nature in him.' Sophie's education, in fact, shows a curious reversion to a sense of that social and psychological pressure from which Émile had been so magnificently released. As a child, she would certainly have more latitude to run about and play and learn things for herself than the orthodox little girl; but she would never be allowed to follow her impulses unchecked. 'Train them to break off their games and return to their other occupations without a murmur. Habit is all that is needed, as you have Nature on your side. This habitual restraint produces a docility which woman requires all her life long, for she will always be in subjection to some man, or to man's judgment, and she will never be free to set her own opinion above his. What is most wanted in a woman is gentleness. Formed to obey a creature so imperfect as man... she should early learn to submit to injustice and to suffer the wrongs inflicted on her by her husband without complaint." . . . "All the reflections of woman which are not immediately concerned with her duties ought to be directed to the study of men, and to those pleasing crafts which have only taste for their object.'

Sophie, thus conventionally brought up to be docile, falls in love with an ideal Émile before she meets him, in the character of Telemachus. There is naturally no trouble when she meets Émile himself.

What *Robinson Crusoe* was to Émile – *Émile* was to Thomas Day. In 1766, two very young men, with queer likenesses and differences, met near Oxford, where one of them was just finishing his course, and the other, an immature husband and father, had recently settled with his family. Day, in appearance very much the unlicked cub who had not yet learnt to comb his hair, was eighteen; Richard Edgeworth was four years older, and, according to Anna Seward, the 'Swan of Lichfield,' 'a young and gay philosopher,' of gracefully spirited address and eloquent conversation who 'danced, fenced and winged his arrows with more than philosophic skill.' They were both young men of fortune, both intelligent, and both suffering from an intellectual infatuation for Rousseau. Edgeworth was already applying *Émile* to his infant son, 'whose body and mind were left as much as possible to the education of nature and accident,' in spite of the protests of friends and relations and the ridicule of outsiders. The child was growing up hardy and fearless; at seven or eight, he knew 'much of things, but less of books' than the ordinary child of four or five. He was bold, free and generous, had keen senses and good judgment. But, except by Edgeworth himself, he was quite unmanageable; he had no manners, and no deference for others. After the child reached the age of eight, the experiment was not pursued; it had too many inconveniences and Edgeworth had other things to do.

Young Day was made of tougher material. His early life had encouraged natural dourness. He was the only son of a widowed mother, who had married again when he was seven, and married unfortunately. Day never got on with his stepfather, whom he later described as a pretentious busy-body, and who was certainly a sponger. The usual remedy of sending the difficult step-son away to school at the earliest possible age was adopted. Even at Charterhouse, Day was the eccentric who would not accept conventions. He avoided 'frivolous amusements', and gave away all his pocket-money. He would not rob birds' nests. But – very necessarily, no doubt – he made himself a first-rate boxer – only to stop and shake hands as soon as he saw that he was winning a fight. At Oxford, where he went at sixteen (a usual age in those days), he carried on the same tradition. He hardly ever touched alcohol, and ate little meat. If he did not comb his hair, he had a habit of bathing in streams – no doubt, the colder, the better. There is no record how he first met Rousseau's theories – they were certainly not included in the University course. *Émile* and *The Social Contract* had been first published when he was fourteen. His meeting with Edgeworth may well have been also his first introduction to Rousseau. In any case, it is clear that Rousseau came to him with that effect of recognition which often makes one particular book almost like a first love to an intelligent adolescent.

Though Day had not had Émile's training, and never could have it now, he was almost as 'alone in human society and counting only upon himself' as any young man well could be. There was, however, one important exception. Until he was twenty-one, his mother was his guardian. At that age he would have complete control of the small fortune left by his father, £1,200 a year (a much larger income then than now), subject to his mother's jointure of £300. The self-dependent Day probably never realised – he was not a subtle thinker – how far social and psychological self-dependence itself may depend upon this highly artificial fact – that, without question or exertion of any kind, £220 will be forthcoming from a Bank every quarter. Naturally, he had always intended to work. His first idea had been to make himself a doctor in order that he might live in some country place and give free treatment to the peasants, while applying his capital to the improvement of agriculture; but he had become disgusted with medicine on learning that it was not an exact science. The incalculability of the human mind and body was always a grievance to Day. His next impulse was a pugnacious one. He would become a lawyer in order to attack legal intricacies from the inside. The law was peculiarly obnoxious to the Rousseau-ist, because it complicated the simple issues of the *Social Contract*, and supported all the superfluous artificial framework of property, class and so on. It was the Law that kept the real men – the peasants and artisans – from enjoying the fruits of their labours and made possible that abomination, 'the fine gentleman.' Day actually read for the Bar and was ultimately called; but he had become very sick of it before that, and never practised. Antagonism is hardly a sufficient force to carry one through years of difficult and tedious study.

Meanwhile, contact with Edgeworth's more volatile mind was working its effect on Day's slow-moving mental machinery. 'A new era in my life,' Edgeworth calls their first meeting; but the sequel shows how much more significant it was for his friend than for himself. To Edgeworth, ideas were playthings, to be handled and used as long as they were amusing and tossed on one side when they become tiresome. The two young men were each other's complements. Day provided a solid basis for Edgeworth to dance on, Edgeworth gave colour and enterprise to Day's solitary cogitations. And, always, throughout their long friendship, it was Edgeworth who scored, as the man less deeply concerned invariably scores. As time went on, Edgeworth became more adaptable, more pliable to conditions, keeping just enough of his early ideas to give him a piquant touch of originality; Day became more and more set upon his own path. Edgeworth was a social success and made the most of it; Day was not. If he had been, would the adventure of his life have been carried through? But the 'sour grapes' theory, in such a case, is too easy. These things grow up slowly. The difficult and unpopular child is compelled to go his own way, but he is probably difficult and unpopular in the first place because he is original. Or, rather, it is the interaction of creature and environment, one of the potent struggles of nature, out of which all life develops. Edgeworth had the pleasanter life: Day produced something significant.

Day was disgusted with the Law; even before his course was finished, he was turning back to a more positive application of his ideal. He would settle on the land, become a peasant among peasants, and live out his theories in action. During his vacations, he tramped the country, studying conditions, staying at the country inns and mixing for preference with the bar patrons. But, first of all, there was a more urgent matter to be settled. It was too late to start as Émile had started, but he had done his best, and it was not too late for the coping-stone of Émile's education. In all essentials, Day clearly felt himself to be Émile. But Émile had been introduced to Sophie at twenty, and this was obviously a matter that should not be any longer deferred. Rousseau was as definite as any theologian that 'it is not good for man to be alone,' and Day agreed with him. Unfortunately, it was also too late to give the destined Sophie the special education which should have begun at birth A marriage between an Émile in the late thirties to a Sophie of seventeen would throw the whole scheme out of gear. This Émile, therefore must rely on happy chance to provide him with a suitable bride. He had set out his requirements in verse:—

> *Health's rosy bloom upon thy cheek,*
> *Eyes that with artless lustre roll,*
> *More eloquent than words to speak*
> *The genuine feelings of the soul.*

> *Such be thy form! Thy noble mind*
> *By no false culture led astray,*
> *By native sense alone refined*
> *In Reason's plain and simple way.*
>
> *Indifferent if the eye of Fame*
> *Thy merit unobserving see;*
> *And heedless of the praise or blame*
> *Of all mankind, of all but me.*
>
> *Sequestered in some secret glade,*
> *With thee unnoticed I would live,*
> *And if content adorn the shade,*
> *What more can Heaven or Nature give?*

In this frame of mind, Day went one summer with his friend Edgeworth to visit the family home in Ireland. On the way, they had an encounter that, in its consequences, provided Day with his future audience.

Now and then, it occurs at some unexpected time and place, that two or three minds above the average appear simultaneously. They find each other with delight, react on, stimulate each other, gather others to them, and create a little culture and civilisation of their own – insignificant enough beside the intellectual life of a great city, but having its own peculiar flavour, none the less. It would probably puzzle a sociologist to explain why Lichfield in the latter half of the eighteenth century should have suddenly become a miniature Athens. Its two most famous sons, Johnson and Garrick, had left it, to be merged in the life of the capital. There remained Dr. Erasmus Darwin, who, like Rousseau, though from another side, had some intuition of the doctrine with which his famous grandson was to revolutionise the intellectual world. Dr. Darwin was a true original, one whose first-hand mind applied itself to medicine, mechanics, botany, agriculture and poetry. His personality, as described by Anna Seward, was curiously like that of Dr. Johnson. He was big, stout, clumsily made, with features 'rather saturnine than sprightly.' A stoop and a full-bottomed wig made him appear elderly even in youth. He had a bad stammer, but 'what he said was always well worth waiting for, though the inevitable impression it made might not always be pleasant to individual self-love.' He was sore upon opposition and revenged it by keen sarcasm; he was extremely sceptical and would achieve his diagnoses by means of a hostile cross-examination very trying to patients. However, since he was always curing them by unorthodox treatments, they soon began to come to him from all over the country. In one case, he seriously considered blood transfusion, although the treatment was then unheard of, and special instruments would have to be made. Anna Seward herself offered to be the donor; but, perhaps fortunately, since 'blood groups' were then unknown, the patient responded to vegetarian diet and the idea was abandoned. On another occasion, Darwin spent the night in a garden to be near a valued patient in a serious condition, since he had not been asked to stay in the house; and passed his time paraphrasing a sonnet of Petrarch. Between Dr. Darwin and Dr. Johnson, 'a mutual and strong dislike subsisted.'

Dr. Darwin set the tone of the Lichfield Circle. It was something fresh – a spirit of experiment, and largely of mechanical experiment, having direct contact with artisanship and craftsmanship, and, in this way, allied to the spirit of Rousseauism. Richard Edgeworth had introduced himself to Darwin after having applied to coach-making a device of his which made the turning of a coach much safer. Apparently, he had not asked permission to do this; but no question of patents or profits seems ever to have arisen, merely a friendship.

Anna Seward supplied the graces of the Lichfield Circle. Her poetry, which won her the title of the 'Swan of Lichfield,' seems to modern taste more like the swan's usual expression than its legendary dying music. But it pleased her contemporaries; and her *Life of Darwin* sufficiently justifies Edgeworth's eulogy on her wit and intelligence.

It was Dr. Darwin whom Edgeworth and Day fell in with on their journey to Ireland. The encounter had the farcical atmosphere that young Edgeworth was apt to create around him. He had drawn Day into one of the meaningless practical jokes which are so amusing to high-spirited youngsters. They put up at a country inn with Day in the character of an eccentric, misanthropic master and Edgeworth as an impudent servant who proceeded to turn the inn upside down. Into the midst of this, arrived Dr. Darwin and shattered the fatuous game by hailing Edgeworth. The three settled down to a more conventional evening. At first, Dr. Darwin was not impressed by Day, but the conversation later on taking a philosophical turn, he changed his mind and Day, too, received his passport into the Lichfield Circle.

It was some time before he took advantage of it. The quest for Sophie was occupying all his energies. At first, he thought he had found her in Edgeworth's sister, Margaret, but that lady had too much of the family *joie de vivre* and did not sufficiently despise the amenities of life. When Day made his proposal, she could only reply that 'she was compelled to acknowledge that, if the gentleman continued a year in the same mind, and could in that time make his appearance becoming a man of his situation, she might be induced to give him her hand.'

Day went away, disgruntled, and before the year was out, the lovers had discovered, as Edgeworth puts it, what all their friends had seen from the beginning, that they were not suited to each other.

But Sophie had to be found. It seemed now to Day that it was useless to look for her in any adult woman, since even Edgeworth's sister had been hopelessly corrupted by society. On the other hand, she could not now be caught in early childhood. But perhaps a compromise might be possible; perhaps he might find someone still young enough to learn, but for whom he would not have to wait too long. Day was now his own master, and had the handling of his money. He put into action 'a scheme which had long occupied his imagination.' With Bicknel, a young barrister friend, he went to a Foundling Home in Shrewsbury, taking testimonials to his moral probity, and selected a young girl of thirteen. Edgeworth, an excellent judge, describes her flatteringly. 'Her countenance was engaging. She had fine auburn hair that hung in natural ringlets on her neck. Her long eyelashes and eyes expressive of sweetness interested all who saw her and the uncommon melody of her voice made a favourable impression upon every person she talked to.' A little hitch occurred. Whatever his moral probity, it was against the rules for a foundling to be adopted by an unmarried man. 'Sabrina' was, therefore, bound apprentice to the absent Edgeworth, who knew nothing of it, but, when he heard, took his responsibility with characteristic lightheartedness. Day, however, did not intend to have all his eggs in one basket. A pretty young blonde, with blue eyes, was spirited in the same manner from the London Foundling Hospital She would share Sabrina's education up to marriageable age and then Day would make his choice, providing suitably for the rejected one.

The story reads like an undergraduate's escapade and, no doubt, there was something of that spirit in it. Day was still barely twenty-two. But then it is just this youthfulness, this experimental spirit – a reckless urge to act out speculations – which constitutes the artist – those elect and troublesome beings who never grow up, never settle down, nor realise that they are the puppets of circumstance and not its masters. If Day had been mere undergraduate, the 'stunt' would have been abandoned, paid for, and huddled out of sight within a few months.

So the youth of twenty-two began the training of his potential brides of twelve and thirteen. At all costs, they must be guarded against corrupting influences. Day considered the matter in all its bearings, and decided that the best plan would be to take them somewhere where they did not know the language and would be cut off from all communication except with their fiancé-tutor. Accordingly, the three set out for France within a few weeks of the adoption, without taking even an English servant.

Day, himself, never described the course of the experiment, much to the loss of posterity. The only sidelights come from Edgeworth and from Anna Seward. Their accounts of the French year differ considerably. Miss Seward suggests a slightly malicious dramatic heightening; Edgeworth's a tempering of regard for his friend and for the principles which he shared. Neither, of course, is a first-hand witness, but Anna Seward is more likely to have had Sabrina's version as well as Day's. According to her, 'they teased and perplexed him; they quarrelled and fought incessantly; they sickened of small-pox; they chained him to their bedside by crying and screaming if they were left with anyone who could not speak to them in English. He came back to England after eight months, heartily glad to separate the little squabblers.'

According to Edgeworth, what Day wanted was merely 'simplicity, perfect innocence and attachment to himself.' To attain these, he reasoned with the children in a manner which Edgeworth thought quite above their heads, though, according to Rousseau, they should now have reached a suitable age for it. By constant ridicule, he tried to make them despise dress, luxury, fine people, fashions and titles.

A letter from Day to Edgeworth tells very little, except that he did not like the French. They were even further from 'natural' simplicity than the English. However, his admiration for *Émile* was unimpaired. If all the books in the world were to be destroyed, he says, the second book he would save, after the Bible, would be *Émile*.

The letter Sabrina dictated is, in its implications, more illuminating:—

'Dear Mr. Edgeworth,—I am glad to hear that you are well, and your little boy – I love Mr. Day dearly and Lucretia – I am learning to write – I do not like France so well as England – The people are very brown, they dress very oddly – I hope I shall have more sense against I come to England – I know how to make a circle and an equilateral triangle – I know the cause of night and day, winter and summer – I love Mr. Day best in the world, Mr. Bicknel next and you next.'

Whether by reason of his disappointment with the French, or his fatigue in the unmitigated society of his wards, Day brought them back to England in 1770. He had decided that one was enough, and Sabrina, his first choice, seemed to him the better subject. Lucretia was accordingly apprenticed to a milliner, where she must quickly have unlearnt the rudiments of her 'natural' education, for she did well and married a prosperous tradesman.

Since isolation in a foreign country had proved unsatisfactory, Day looked round for the best environment he could find for the completion of Sabrina's training, and remembered that he had the freedom of a select Circle in which, even if the members had not had the benefit of a natural education, they were at least intelligent and open-minded. So the rest of the experiment was carried out under enquiring eyes. Day took a house in the Stow valley and set up housekeeping.

It is a tribute to his personality, as Edgeworth remarks, even in that enlightened society, that 'his breeding up of a young girl in his house, without any female to take care of her, created no scandal, and appeared quite natural and free of impropriety.'

The Lichfield Circle were interested and friendly, if also a little amused. Anna Seward describes Day at this first introduction. 'Mr. Day looked the philosopher. Powder and fine clothes were at that time the appendages of a gentleman. Day wore not either. He was tall and stooped in the shoulders, full-made, but not corpulent, and, in his meditative and melancholy air, a degree of awkwardness and dignity were blended. We found his features interesting and agreeable amidst the traces of a severe small-pox. There was a sort of weight upon the lids of his large hazel eyes.'

Miss Seward describes the progress of the experiment with some insight. Poor Sabrina was disappointing. 'Her spirit could not be armed against the dread of pain and the appearance of danger. When he dropped melted sealing-wax on her arms she did not endure it heroically, nor when he fired pistols at her petticoats which she believed charged with balls' (the experiment is recommended by the Master – but for Émile, not for Sophie), 'could she help starting aside or suppress her screams.'

But the critical test came when Day told her 'secrets about well-invented dangers to himself in which greater danger would result from its being discovered that he was aware of them.' It presently became evident that Sabrina had passed on these fatal secrets to servants and playfellows. Discretion was a vital virtue for Sophie, and it began to be clear to Day that his chosen one would never be a Sophie.

He endured it, says Anna Seward, for a year. It is more surprising that Sabrina endured it. The ladies of the Circle had been kind to her. She was a frequent guest at the Bishops' Palace where the Sewards lived. Experimental zeal and human sympathy must surely sometimes have been at war in the minds of the bevy of cultured women who graced the household; but there is no record of any attempt at interference. The real trouble, says the chronicler, was to give Sabrina a motive for exertion, self-dependence and heroism. Pecuniary reward, luxury, ambition, vanity were all ruled out by Day's system. There remained attachment to her benefactor. But Sabrina was afraid of Day.

A year after the settlement in Lichfield, Sabrina was sent to a boarding-school in Sutton-Coldfield. Perhaps, as Miss Seward says, Day had given her up; perhaps, as Edgeworth suggests, even he had begun to feel the unsuitability of his ménage, as Sabrina grew older. But the sequel shows that another factor was also coming into play.

Day was now twenty-three; and it had evidently become something of a strain to wait for Sophie. Émile had met his Sophie when he was twenty and she was already a finished product. Certainly, Émile had been taken a little into society for two or three years previously, but his practical mind had, of course, disdained the artificial graces that he found there. This is one of the points at which one begins to question Rousseau's psychology. Would the savage, however noble, inevitably be proof against all the ladies he might meet in the salons? Is it human nature, even uncorrupted human nature, always to prefer the natural? At least, this older Émile, though fortified by conscious intention, did not escape unscathed from the Lichfield salons.

With the Sewards was living a motherless girl, Honora Sneyd. Edgeworth is eloquent about her. 'For the first time in my life,' he says, 'I saw a woman that equalled that picture of perfection which existed in my imagination.'

Honora was generally admired, though a little overshadowed by the great Anna. Only Day had appeared blind to the 'superiority of her character.' 'She danced too well, she had too much an air of fashion in her dress and manners, and her arms were not sufficiently round and white to please him.'

Edgeworth did not conceal his own feelings about Honora, but Edgeworth was already married. He did not conceive himself happily married. 'I had long suffered from the want of that cheerfulness in a wife without which marriage could not be agreeable to such a temper as mine. I had borne this trial with patience, but my not being happy at home exposed me to the danger of being too happy elsewhere.' On Honora's side, already, when Edgeworth left Lichfield in 1770, she had 'seemed to feel that I was the first person who had seen the full value of her character.'

But Edgeworth went reluctantly back to Ireland and domestic duty. And Day, disappointed by his failure with Sabrina, soon began to progress from the slight aversion which is said to be the best beginning. Honora herself was in the position of having just lost two lovers, the ineligible Edgeworth, and Major André, who was also, for some reason, considered unsuitable.

In a very short time, Day was writing to Edgeworth pointing out to him the folly and meanness of a hopeless passion for any woman, but assuring him that 'he would never marry so as to divide himself from his chosen friend.' In short, could Edgeworth stand it, if he proposed to Honora? Edgeworth's reaction was one that he would probably have hesitated to record if he had lived in these latter days of psychological analysis. The best way to find out if he could stand it, he thought, would be to come and see. He came, and decided that he could enthusiastically assist in Day's wooing.

The next morning, Day delivered to him 'in a very solemn manner,' some sheets of paper which contained a proposal of marriage and a plan of life. It embodied points that he had already discussed with Honora, he told Edgeworth, and, if she once agreed to join him in a calm, secluded life, he was convinced that she would never wish to return to more gay and splendid scenes. Edgeworth delivered the packet to Honora and was told to return the next morning for the answer. When it came, Day read it alone, and when, after a tactful interval, Edgeworth came back, he found him in a fever. The letter was shown to him. It contained, he says, an excellent answer to Day's arguments. Miss Sneyd objected to the unqualified control of a husband. (No doubt, she had seen something of Sabrina's training.) She did not consider seclusion necessary to female virtue or to domestic happiness. In short, she did not intend to change her present mode of living for 'any dark and untried system.'

Edgeworth implies that this answer was as much a surprise to himself as to Day. And there is nothing to show that his conduct in the matter was not as magnanimous as it appears on the surface. But the best of human motives are apt to be mixed and, when he remarks that Day, unlike himself, was not a man of strong passions, one cannot help reflecting that this must have been a very convenient belief for Edgeworth. To measure the force of passions, it is necessary to consider the strength of the control as well as of the impulse. On this occasion, however, Day had a real illness. He was in bed for some days and Dr. Darwin came to bleed and to scold him.

Day was not allowed to seclude himself after his misfortune. The Lichfield Circle was too small, and, no doubt, it would have been against his principles to permit such a set-back to interfere with his habits. But the need to find Sophie was becoming more and more merged in the more general, human need to find a wife. His own nature at this point shows signs of taking charge of the carefully schooled Child of Nature. For his next choice was even more unlikely.

The Sneyd family settled in Lichfield about this time, and Honora rejoined them. With the rest, came her young sister, Elizabeth, a person regarded by the Circle as of less solid worth than Honora, but very gay, charming and a natural coquette.

Elizabeth was not so graceful as Honora, and was not fond of dancing. This was in her favour. Also, she did not argue; her conversational powers shone best in the small change of social intercourse, and, when graver subjects were under discussion, she was content to be a good listener. It soon became clear that, as Edgeworth puts it, Elizabeth had made a greater impression in three weeks upon Mr. Day than her superior sister had made in twelve months. Elizabeth, too, was impressed. She found a fascination in the odd, serious young man with a plan of life. His idea that husband and wife should be all in all to each other and indifferent to the rest of the world appealed to her young romanticism. At the same time, it would be pleasanter to have a husband whom one could introduce to one's friends without misgiving. She could not quite accept Day as he was, but she could not bring herself to shut the door altogether. She put the matter otherwise than Honora, though probably not precisely in Miss Seward's Johnsonian diction – 'that if he would acquire the manners of the outside world, instead of his austere singularities of air, habit, and address, she could have loved him.'

This frivolous objection now seemed to Day less insuperable than Honora's assertion of Woman's Rights. Elizabeth's mind might still be formed on important matters, if he gave way a little on superficial ones. After all, Rousseau had at last introduced Émile himself into Society, and, unlike his more romantic followers, had expected him to adapt himself sensibly, so that he would be unobtrusively popular, though, of course, never gulled by fashionable values. And there was something in the argument which Edgeworth attributes to Elizabeth, that Day 'could not with propriety abuse and ridicule talent in which he appeared obviously deficient.'

A bargain was struck. Day would go to France for a year and learn to be a fine gentleman. Elizabeth, meanwhile, would not go to London, or Bath, or any other place of public amusement.

In the meantime, Edgeworth and Honora were again finding propinquity dangerous. Day took his friend in hand and persuaded him to go with him on his year of probation.

There is a little perhaps natural malice in Edgeworth's account of the experiment. In Lyons, Day 'put himself to every species of torture, ordinary and extraordinary, to compel his antigallican limbs, in spite of their natural rigidity, to dance, and fence and manage the *great horse*.' His energy and perseverance astonished his friend. He would stand for hours in a machine designed to straighten the knees. It was all in vain. Day was twenty-four and his joints were set, no less than his mental habits. Edgeworth pitied his poor friend, 'with his feet in the stocks, a book in his hand and contempt in his heart.'

Edgeworth meanwhile found, as usual, congenial society and undertook an engineering job connected with the diversion of the Rhone for the enlargement of Lyons. Fortified by a visit from his family, he was well content to stay out of danger when Day had completed his year's immolation and went back to hear his fate.

Anna Seward takes up the melancholy chronicle. The Lichfield Circle was anything but overwhelmed by the newly made Fine Gentleman. They had liked and admired their oddity, even while they laughed at him. They did not like this new hybrid from Lyons. The visible effort of holding himself erect was more really ungraceful than the natural stoop. The studied bow, the sudden assumption of attitude, 'prompted the risible instead of the admiring sensation.' The showy dress did not suit him. Elizabeth had to confess that Day 'the blackguard' had appealed to her more than Day, the fine gentleman. Probably she was also tired of refraining from London and from Bath. Day found that he had made a fool of himself for nothing, and very quickly shook off the effects of his French year.

Not long afterwards the first Mrs. Edgeworth died in childbirth. Edgeworth came posting home. In France, he had heard that Honora had eye trouble which might end in the loss of her sight, but, as he naïvely announces, as soon as he heard of his wife's death, he had made up his mind to marry her, even if she were totally blind. He was met on the road by Day, who was determined to be the first to tell him that Honora was in perfect health, more beautiful and more sought after than ever, but still free. Within a year, Honora had become the second Mrs. Edgeworth.

It would have been unthinkable to Day that he should in any way resent his friend's happiness. He certainly had no logical right to do so. And he was the man who had endowed for life the step-father who had bullied him, in order to set his mother's mind at rest. Nowadays, schooled by modern psychology, we do not expect so much of ourselves, thus making it quite certain that we shall not get it. We have another idea of 'Nature' than Day's, and know that jealousy and malice are innate instincts, magnanimity and self-sacrifice, worthless shams. Even Day was not superhuman, and a certain reaction from that generous rush to tell his friend the good news may be read between the lines of his congratulatory letter. We can take our choice whether to regard the letter as it stands as a piece of heroism or a piece of stupid self-deception. Or perhaps the two are not incompatible. At least, the friendship survived.

In a somewhat disillusioned strain, he wishes Edgeworth all happiness. He himself is more inclined than ever to withdraw from human intercourse. Their affection will remain as strong as ever, but their habitual intercourse will, in the nature of things, be somewhat diminished. He did what little he could for Edgeworth when he was in trouble and confided to him his own youthful hopes and schemes of happiness. Now, his own tendency to Stoicism, joined with the change in Edgeworth's circumstances, must necessarily make them of less active importance to each other. Edgeworth will be stationary, himself a wanderer. 'An indifference to all human affairs, an aversion to restraint and engagement and embarrassment continue to increase in my mind.' He has decided that he is marked out by fate to be a bachelor and an eccentric, destined perhaps to become very old, 'because I am very indifferent about the matter, and to buy hobby horses for your grandchildren.'

The last paragraph adds, 'Pray, to Mrs. Edgeworth, say from me everything that may best express the real friendship and esteem I have for her, and the conviction that, so far from being any obstacle to our future friendship, she will always entertain for me such sentiments as I deserve for my behaviour to her husband.'

When the Edgeworths settled in England, Day was nevertheless a frequent visitor. He had abandoned Lichfield; no doubt, that eager audience had by this time proved too much for even his nerves. He was living at the Temple, writing pamphlets and poems and making frequent excursions over England on foot, carrying on his social studies. The quest for Sophie had been temporarily abandoned.

But, at twenty-five, even the most confirmed misanthrope does not settle down to a lonely old age. Sabrina was coming on. It presently occurred to Day that perhaps he had abandoned the struggle too soon. Here, at least, was a young girl, still unformed in many ways, who was completely dependent upon him. His letters to Edgeworth began to be full of her again, recounting her sayings and doings and, above all, the progress of her mind. Edgeworth did not think that her mind would ever amount to much, but, as a young piece of femininity, he evidently appreciated her. At this time, he thought that she was in love with Day. It might be the best solution, after all. Clearly, Day would never win a woman of culture; the Child of Nature, even if he had sometimes wandered from his path, had at least succeeded in unfitting himself for that. But he might still have a woman who, if she could not talk to him, could at least listen submissively.

And then, in a moment, it was all over. There is real impatience in Edgeworth's account of it. Day had left Sabrina at the house of a friend, with strict injunctions as to some particular fancies of his own, some restrictions as to her dress. 'She neglected, or forgot, or undervalued something which was not, I believe, clearly defined. She did, or did not, wear certain long sleeves, and some handkerchief which had been the subject of his dislike or his liking; and he, considering this circumstance as a criterion of her attachment and as a proof of her want of strength of mind, quitted her for ever.' Day's letter, he says, convinced him that, with his peculiarities, he had judged well for his happiness; 'but . . . I could not have acted as he did.'

Sabrina, however, did not become the third Mrs. Edgeworth. That fate was reserved for Elizabeth Sneyd. Sabrina married Mr. Bicknel, who left her a penniless widow with two young sons, a few years later.

Day had not been alone in his quest for Sophie. He had a benevolent friend, a Dr. Small of Birmingham, who was always looking round for him, and constantly bringing up candidates. While Day was dallying with Sabrina again, he had found one whom he thought excellent, and, now that Sabrina was finally abandoned, he introduced the subject. Edgeworth records the conversation, whether from first-hand knowledge, report, or imagination, there is nothing to show.

The lady was Esther Milnes, a Yorkshire woman of

private fortune, intelligent and cultured, philanthropic, and with a strong preference for the solid virtues as against the lighter graces.

'But has she white and large arms?' said Mr. Day. It was the one aesthetic qualification on which he always insisted.

'She has,' replied Dr. Small.

'Does she wear long petticoats?'

'Uncommonly long.'

'I hope she is tall and strong and healthy.'

'Remarkably little and not robust. My good friend,' added Dr. Small, speaking in his leisurely manner. 'Can you possibly expect that a woman of charming temper, benevolent, with views of life congenial to your own, with an agreeable person and a large fortune, should be found exactly according to a picture that exists in your imagination? . . . If you are not satisfied, determine at once never to marry.'

'My dear doctor,' replied Mr. Day, 'the only serious objection which I have to Miss Milnes is her large fortune. It was always my wish to give any woman I married the most unequivocal proof of my attachment by despising her fortune.'

'Well, my friend,' said the Doctor, 'What prevents you from despising the fortune and taking the lady?'

Day went to Yorkshire and at last found Sophie. She was cultured; she had literary tastes; she had money – all bad points; but she had the essential – that willingness – eagerness – to submit to male domination which was Sophie's mainspring. She had no use for fashionable graces. She wanted a man whose character she could respect, who would tell her what to do and what to think. She was prepared to love him in a cottage, if he preferred it.

The courtship was leisurely and philosophical. All

important questions had to be discussed and disposed of. 'I believe,' said Edgeworth, 'that few lovers ever conversed or corresponded more. At last they were married.'

At thirty, Day had thus completed the essential preliminary to the life that he had planned. It was now a question of starting upon that life. He set about the matter with his usual deliberation. While they were looking about for a suitable farm on which to settle, they lodged in Hampstead in quarters that seemed to Edgeworth quite unnecessarily small and uncomfortable. He surmised that Day wished to break his wife in to the Simple Life. Edgeworth and Honora visited them there and were surprised to find them walking over the Heath in the snow, Mrs. Day being protected by a frieze cloak and thick shoes. However, he admits that her health seemed all the better for the treatment.

'I never saw any woman so entirely intent upon accommodating herself to the sentiments and wishes and will of her husband,' he remarks, and describes, with a touch of malice, Mrs. Day's way with her husband and mentor. Apparently, Day's habit of making disquisitions on everything that came up, from political questions to the trivial occurrences of everyday life, never bored her. She would put in just enough comment and even divergence of sentiment to stimulate him, and never enough to annoy him. Mrs. Day was evidently the rare type of clever woman who is content to grace a second place well.

The farm on which Day decided to settle and begin the living of the 'Simple Life' was at Stapleford Abbots in Essex. Edgeworth had urged him to settle near himself in Hertfordshire; but Day, he thought, was afraid of exposing his wife to other influences than his own. Probably (though this Edgeworth does not add) he had not forgotten Honora's eloquent statement of the Rights of Women. The house at Stapleford Abbots was indifferent, and the land, worse. Day made up his mind to extend the house, and, in preparation, read Ware's *Architecture*. He intended to do the work himself, but a week convinced him that he was not suited to the mason's craft. It deranged his walks and discussions with Mrs. Day, and prevented his concentration on his books. The years that he had spent in studying for the 'Simple Life' had, in fact, made a bookworm and a pedagogue of Day. Or, perhaps, the difference goes deeper. Émile had been the 'natural man,' in acting unconsciously; but to try consciously to be natural, and still more to try to make other people so, is, after all, a highly artificial enterprise. Books and theory had become Day's element; and, now, the 'Simple Life' had to be combined with them. He left the completion of his house to the builders, and was so irritated when one of them interrupted him to ask about the position of a window, that the room was built without any window at all and came to be used only as a box-room.

The 'Simple Life' was lived chiefly in deprivation. Mrs. Day, says Anna Seward, pityingly, had to do without a carriage, and without any personal service. Music, in which she had been proficient, was ruled out as trivial; and her harpsichord and music books were banished. Miss Seward adds that there were frequent experiments on her temper and attachments, over which 'she sometimes wept, but never repined.' Mrs. Day, however, seems to have been a reincarnation of Patient Griselda. Her fortune had been settled on her at her marriage, but she never made any use of it except in benefactions.

The Stapleford Abbots experiment proved unsatisfactory and the Days moved to another farm in Surrey three years later. Day was still determined to make it as hard for himself as possible. 'One of the most unprofitable farms in England,' Edgeworth called it. But Day thought it gave all the more scope for improvement

and for doing good to his neighbours. He had shifted
from Rousseau's point of view that man must work on
what he finds and win his living from it. Rousseau, no
more than any modern industrialist, would have approved
of working on something that could not be made to pay its
way. Day still regarded the peasantry 'as the stamina of
the human species,' from which all the other degenerate
ranks of society must in the end be recruited, but he was
illogically content to do them good from the outside. He
poured his private fortune into developing the Surrey
estate. He gave all the employment he could, whether it
was economically justifiable or not, and alienated the
local farmers by paying higher wages in winter when there
was little work to be done, because the labourers needed it
more. Helped by his wife, he gave what seemed to him
judicious charity on a large scale, held classes and even
Sunday services for the villagers, since the church was
three miles away.

Day was quickly on bad terms with most of his neighbours. His competition in the labour market seemed to
them unfair. They despised his way of living. One local
squire wrote him a letter warning him against the sin of
avarice. He got the reputation of a misanthrope. He
held his position, because he had the necessary money,
but the reputation of misanthropy, as far as his own class
was concerned, seems to have been justified. The estate
at Anningsley was a wilderness when he bought it; the
house itself, to an impressionable observer, seemed 'shy
and mysterious, peeping at the wild solitary world
beyond,' and away from the land that Day himself had
improved. Day tried to turn his back on the social world
in the same manner. He had gone there, he told a friend,
'to exclude myself from the vanity, vice and deceptive
character of man.' As time went on, the little household
became more and more concentrated on itself and on its

activities among the peasants. There are bitter letters to Edgeworth describing and philosophising on the ingratitude and incurable levity of the human species, against false friends, and stating that he believed it a mistake ever to give pecuniary help to anyone. He admits, evidently in answer to Edgeworth's accusation, that his attitude to the world has become defensive. He has found it necessary.

At the same time, he claimed that he was happy. The study of agriculture, constant business, outdoor life, the caring for men and animals, saved him from solitary stagnation, he said; and in this way he was able to live happily independently of his fellow-creatures without fatigue or boredom.

That he was not, however, quite happy without some contact with the outer world seems evident from the fact that he sought the more remote contact of literature. Every public event and movement during these years brought a tract from his pen. He protested against the American War, against slavery, against customs duties, against the Warren Hastings trial, against the taxation of farmers. He even made some tentative excursions into politics, and Pitt's party would have supported his candidature for Parliament. But seats in Parliament could at that time be had only by buying them, and, for Day, that put a parliamentary career out of the question.

All his books but one are excessively dull. And that book was not a political tract; it was *Sandford and Merton*, Day's *Émile*. The hero is the child in Day that had never grown up, set in a small world where Right and 'Nature' always triumph. Little Harry Sandford scores again and again over the little 'fine gentleman' the victories that Day had failed to score in life. He rescues Tommy Merton when he is lost; saves him from the bull which he has unregenerately gone to see baited; shows him how to build a shack in case they should ever be cast on a desert island; looks disdainfully at the trappings and silver of his fine house and says he prefers their own horn mugs, because one need not worry if anyone drops them; magnanimously saves the life of the squire who has beaten him for not telling which way the hare went; and wins the affectionate esteem of Miss Simmons, the only sensible little girl in Tommy's court of miniature ladies and gentlemen. At last, the little gentleman is converted.

'I shall not be long without you,' he says, taking the farmer's son by the hand. 'To your example I owe most of the little good that I can boast; you have taught me how much better it is to be useful than rich and fine – how much more amiable to be good than great. Should I be ever tempted to relapse, even for an instant, into any of my former habits, I will return hither for instruction and I hope you will again receive me.'

But the squires of Surrey did not take Day by the hand, nor make any such pretty speeches. Whether he would have remained content with the armed neutrality of his own life in the world, and the imaginary triumphs of Harry Sandford, must be left an unsolved problem, for he was spared the misgivings and belated efforts of later middle life by an early martyrdom. His theories extended to the breaking of horses by kindness, and this, too, he put into practice. The young subject of the experiment shied and threw him. Day fell on his head, never recovered consciousness, and so died at the age of forty-one.

Day's interested contemporaries did not know what to make of him. Most of them were never sure whether he was the hero or the clown. Edgeworth, the most intelligent, escapes in his usual manner by externalising the conflict. He had intended to write Day's life, but found himself forestalled by another friend. But the lively passages in the *Memoirs* almost amount to a biography.

In the last of them, his qualms appear. Almost, he feels, he has done Day a wrong in making his sketch, betrayed confidences and acted as a false friend. But everyone intimately concerned is dead; and he thinks he has been justified in drawing as accurately as he could, a portrait that may be useful to others. If he has shown that one may have 'too much of a good thing,' even of reason and deliberation, his object has not been to ridicule Day.

Keir, the actual biographer, produced a book that is an extended tombstone epitaph. He touches very lightly on the Sabrina and Lucretia episode, and never mentions the affairs with Honora and Elizabeth Sneyd.

Patient Griselda's comment was more poignant. She moped for two years, never going out in the daytime, and was uncheered even by a letter from Edgeworth, pointing out that he, too, had lost a beloved spouse, yet had taken up his life again (he had now passed on to Elizabeth Sneyd), and was even enjoying it, as he knew his dear one would have wished. However, Mrs. Day preferred to die instead.

But, to the general eye and the eye of posterity, Day remained something of a comic figure. It was inevitable that he should be laughed at, because he was one of the rare persons who do not act, or refrain from action for fear of being laughed at. His reward was to achieve a coherence in his life which is apt to be lacking in the lives of people of humour and adaptability.

ACKNOWLEDGMENTS

In Section IV, the quotations from Rousseau's *Émile*, on pages 141, 142, lines 7–18, are from the translation published by Dent in the Everyman edition.

V

THE FREE WOMAN

IN 1821, at Nohant, in the French province of Bas-Berry, a young woman of seventeen got thoroughly out of hand. In a small way, she was an important young woman. She was the sole heiress of the estate of Nohant, and her grandmother had just died, leaving her in possession of the château and land where she had grown up in the rôle of the young squire. It was a pleasant little property. An eighteenth century mansion had been built in 1767 on the ruins of an old castle. The high road passed near by, screened off by tall trees and a shrubbery. Around the gates clustered the tiny dependent village of Nohant with its church, and, in the château itself, lived always a horde of servants and hangers-on, from Aurore Dupin's illegitimate brother to the labourers on the estate. The countryside was flat, with huge fields and rows of pollard willows, an excellent country for riding. Young Aurore had ridden it ever since she could sit a pony, in breeches, smock and gaiters, with two big dogs at her heels. Her grandfather had been a disciple of Rousseau, and his principles of 'natural education' had so far survived him that she had been allowed to mix freely with the peasants and to grow up a complete tomboy to the age of fourteen. When a friend of her grandmother's, temporarily in charge, had tried once to put her into corsets, she had run away and cut the laces, and, when they were replaced, had hurled the whole abomination into a thicket. Her tutor had been a middle-aged man who combined classical and medical knowledge with the stewardship of the estate, played the flageolet and believed in the equality of the sexes.

As, by the time Aurore reached the age of fourteen, this education was showing somewhat chaotic results, her grandmother had taken her to a convent in Paris, where she had spent the next two and a half years. There, she had passed with unusual flamboyance through various schoolgirl phases – ringleadership, midnight prowls to find the walled-up skeleton, adoration for one of the nuns, a violent conversion, and an ambition to become a nun herself. Throughout her childhood and youth, an imaginary companion, Corambé, had accompanied her – an ideal being, whose characteristics varied to suit whatever phase she happened to be passing through.

Back at Nohant, she had turned her devastating vitality to an orgy of miscellaneous reading, having – a little dampingly – been given permission by her confessor to study philosophy, since she would not, he said, go deep enough to do any harm. She also took lessons in surgery, and used the skeleton of a child for purposes of study, though she kept dreaming that it got up and drew her curtains at night.

The local squirearchy had watched all these proceedings with misgiving, especially in view of a still worse fact behind them. Aurore was not pure bred. She was the child of a misalliance. Her father had married the daughter of a Paris bird-fancier, and then died, when Aurore was four, leaving the consequences of his mistakes to other people. Mme. Dupin had been a very difficult consequence. The aristocratic old grandmother could not always keep her away from her little daughter, and, from time to time, the hysterical Parisian demi-mondaine had descended upon Nohant, bringing storms, quarrels, passionate embraces and every kind of drama into Aurore's life. Aurore herself had the natural weakness of her temperament for the losing side; she and her mother had often made wild romantic plans for going away together, throwing up all that Nohant had to offer, and earning their living, if only they could be together. Then Mme. Dupin would have a reaction of French practicality, and go off alone again to her gay life in Paris, leaving the child in bewildered misery.

Now, at seventeen, Aurore was left alone at Nohant, and her grandmother had passed on her responsibility to René de Villeneuve, a local squire and a distant kinsman of the family. Aurore's guardian turned at once to the remedy that naturally suggested itself. The only hope with a turbulent young woman like Aurore was obviously to get her married as quickly as possible. And, since there was no sense in letting the Nohant estate pass out of the family, he proposed his son for the rôle of Petruchio. But he had reckoned without Mme. Dupin. She descended with banners flying, prepared to carry all before her, now that her arch-enemy had been removed for ever. If only Aurore had been of age, it would have been perfect. As it was, there was a scene at the reading of the will. Aurore's guardian and her mother fought over her body. Then M. Villeneuve made a fatal mistake. He told Aurore that, unless she would agree never to see her mother again, the proposals for his son must be considered withdrawn.

Aurore defied her guardian and all the Bas-Berry squirearchy. She would never, she said, marry a man who would not have her mother in the house. The two went off to Paris to the life together they had so long planned.

Poor Aurore quickly found herself in the position of the animal that cannot live in the water and dies on land.

Life in her mother's apartment in Paris turned out to be very different from life at Nohant and still more different from life at the convent. But the spiritual conditions were even more impossible than the material ones. Mme. Dupin was Bohemian in her tastes, excitable and vulgar. She perpetually made scenes. She preyed emotionally on every one who came near her. Constant quarrels and passionate reconciliations were her daily bread. But Aurore took it all seriously. Every quarrel and every reconciliation shook her to her depths. She pined for country air and exercise and for easy-going companionship – always a vital necessity to people who are themselves naturally intense. A few months of it nearly shattered her.

It was out of the question to eat her words and go back to Nohant. And it is very difficult to be original in action at eighteen, still more if one is a woman and living in an age when the social pressure upon women is still strong. Only one way out suggested itself to Aurore – the same way as that which had suggested itself to her guardian. Some old friends of her father's whom she met in Paris saw and pitied her dilemma, and, when she went to stay with them, introduced her to Casimir Dudevant, the natural son and adopted heir of a Gascon Baron of the Empire. Dudevant was of Aurore's own class on her father's side, a country squire with the country squire's tastes. He was good-looking, cheerful and unexactingly friendly. He liked riding and he smelt of the country. Aurore was aware that, in a sense, she was throwing herself away when she agreed to marry him, for he was clearly not a man of culture, but then she thought that she would be able to educate him. At worst, it was a way of 'getting back,' without a humiliating recantation, even with something of a flourish.

For nine years, from 1822 to 1831, the future George Sand was a faithful wife and housekeeper. The fact is apt to lose its true proportion, in view of the more exciting phases of her later life. But nine years is a long time, and it is considerably longer when it runs between the ages of eighteen and twenty-seven than at any subsequent period. Two children were born, Maurice in 1823 and Solange in 1828, and Aurore was a devoted mother to them. It was not, in every way, however, a normal French ménage. Dudevant's father was still alive, and the couple settled at Nohant and lived on its revenues, so that there was always something of the Prince Consort in the young husband's situation. He did not allow the fact to interfere with his habits. On the intellectual side, he quickly proved unamenable to education; when Aurore sat down to the piano, he would go out of the room. His own tastes became grosser as time went on; like most country squires, he drank too much; and he found a congenial companion in Aurore's half-brother, Hippolyte. He was spasmodically unfaithful to her. Violence came natural to him, and, when Aurore became excited in a children's romp, as she was apt to become, and threw some gravel at him, he boxed her ears. Aurore had always a strong sense of personal dignity, and the incident started a smouldering rebellion. She took refuge from the drunken orgies at Nohant in her feudal status with the peasants, went about doctoring them, ordering their affairs, saving them from conscription and pacifying their feuds. In search of mental sustenance, she drew together a small salon from the brighter spirits in the local town of La Châtre and from the Parisians who occasionally came to visit them. Dudevant resented all this and still more the implied assumption of superiority. He did not like a wife whom people thought eccentric. He was still more nonplussed when she wrote him a confession that she had a Platonic lover, Aurélien de Sèze, whom they had met on a holiday in the Pyrenees, and a dramatic statement that they had pledged themselves never to degrade their love by a commonplace liaison.

This spiritual relationship sustained Aurore for three years, and, long afterwards, she was not sure that it had not, after all, been the greatest love of her life. It was a love carried on chiefly in imagination; the lovers met only once or twice in the course of a year, and their letters, which, by the compact which Aurore had forced upon her dismayed husband, were always read by him, confined themselves to everyday matters. It died a natural death when Aurélien began to find it too spiritual, and felt that the step from the sublime to the ridiculous had been taken when he found Aurore sewing baby-clothes in preparation for Solange. Aurore claimed later that she had let him go in peace. She felt that she had become either a 'terrible chain' to him or a 'mental amusement,' and did not seem to be sure which. In any case, 'one should no more dispute the possession of a soul than of a slave.'

But this Madame Bovary had intellect and determination as well as imagination. Aurélien's defection wakened her. Her religion, which her confessor had judged safe from the assaults of philosophy, had by this time, begun to suffer the more deadly attacks of experience. She was trapped in a life that she did not like and felt to be wrong, worn out by 'gaiety without expansion, domesticity without intimacy, solitude that noise and drunkenness rendered more absolute.'

Her loathing of it was developing into a spiritual claustrophobia. Yet her Christian duty was obvious – to stay where she was as a faithful wife, bear meekly with her husband's conduct, look after her children and console herself with pious practices. George Sand always claimed that she was deeply religious, and so far as that state of mind implies an urgent desire to feel right with the universe in general and with herself, she was obviously telling the truth. Yet it was impossible to be content any longer with life at Nohant as Casimir Dudevant's wife. It followed that the religion that bound one to such slavery must be fundamentally wrong. And if the guidance of the Church was wrong, what other guidance was there? Aurore had gradually come to the conclusion, as she explains in the section of her autobiography headed *Du Mysticisme à l'Indépendance* that there is no true guidance but that of intuition. 'I neither could, nor would, act other than in virtue of a law superior to custom and opinion.' 'It was of the greatest importance to me to seek in God, the key to the enigma of my life, the notion of my real duties, the sanction of my most intimate sentiments.' For her, there were always three terms to her spiritual existence, God, He, and I. In this new trinity, the first and third persons always, in the last resort, outweighed the second; and only mystic consultations with the God within her were henceforth to exercise control over Aurore's thoughts and actions. A critic of her novels put it in words often applied to herself. 'In George Sand, when a lady wishes to change her lover, God is always there to facilitate the transfer.'

The epigram is, like most epigrams, a cruel half-truth. That George Sand 'meant well' is as clear as that she caused a vast amount of disturbance and suffering. She followed her impulses, but they were often generous and, even, sometimes self-sacrificing impulses. 'If I have drifted or erred,' she wrote later, 'I have, at least, the great consolation of being certain to-day that I have never acted after reflection, except with the conviction that I am accomplishing a duty or exercising an authentic right, which is, at bottom, the same thing.' A footnote emphasises the point, 'Yes, it is the same thing. One recoils sometimes, before the duty of defending one's right in an impulse of unreflective generosity. I have often done it, perhaps through weakness, and the result has never been good for other people.'

Nevertheless, if one discards codes of conduct, one's own desires transform themselves with an alarming facility into these 'authentic rights.' They are so much nearer and more vivid than other people's desires. Moreover, to decide afresh upon every situation on its merits uses up an enormous amount of vitality. It is an exhausting whole-time job. William James pointed out how greatly nervous energy is economised by automatic actions – what a strain it would be, for instance, if one had to decide every morning which shoe to put on first. Codes of conduct and of manners perform something the same office in the moral sphere. To the person who is impulsive on principle, every situation has to be dealt with afresh, while, to the normally conventional one, it is only necessary to take fresh stock in serious crises. And the mere fact that potentialities of behaviour are unsettled seems itself to give rise to crises. In people of settled principles, erratic little impulses die at birth; others know what to expect of them, they know what to expect of themselves, and disturbances keep their distance. George Sand's life was a series of crises; she attracted them to her.

There is, in short, no more difficult code of conduct than to have none, and this was the enterprise on which Aurore Dudevant embarked when, at the age of twenty-seven, she left her husband, and went to live alone in Paris.

Practical arrangements had naturally caused some difficulty. In law, Aurore's property belonged to her husband. For some time she had been going about with the 'twelve-pound look.' But it was not, in those days, simply a question of buying a typewriter. She had to find a talent in a line open to women that would bring in money. She tried many, probable and improbable, translations, watercolours, sewing, millinery. While she was still looking around, the situation exploded. She came upon a letter of her husband's addressed to herself and to be opened after his death. Seeing no reason why she should wait, Aurore opened it and found all the things that he had wished to say to her and had not dared.

The letter put into her hands the weapon that she had needed. She insisted upon an allowance. 'I must have an alimony. I shall go to Paris. My children shall stay at Nohant,' she repeated again and again at a stormy interview. Dudevant's inevitable impulse was to save appearances at all costs, so far as they could still be saved – in his code, his own behaviour did not matter, but a wife whom he could not manage was the ultimate disgrace. He gave way on the question of the allowance, and of the departure to Paris, so long as the break was not to be immediately final.

Aurore no longer felt any necessity to consider her husband's feelings, but there was the more poignant question of the children. She was genuinely fond of them, and moreover – what, to her dramatic temperament, was perhaps even more important – she always 'saw herself' in the rôle of mother. But it could not fill her life, and she must go to the first duty of all, the development of her personality. To desert her children altogether was equally out of the question. This dilemma threw a tactful vagueness over the departure that was actually so decisive.

Aurore agreed that she would still spend six months of the year at Nohant. But for this first six months, now, she was going to Paris.

There is, nevertheless, an actual practical difficulty in leaving adrift two children who have been dependent on one for their meals and their medicine, getting up and going to bed, the direction of their play and their lessons – a difficulty that has notoriously held together many an otherwise disrupting household. Maurice was eight and Solange, three. There must be someone to look after them. A problem which was often to recur faced Aurore. She was intermittently conscious of it. 'How are we to make other people's wishes agree with our own desires?' she wrote to her mother. 'I do not know.' But now someone else's wishes had to be made to agree, at all costs. There was a young man who had been Maurice's tutor and who understood him and the ways of the household. Aurore had mothered him while he was with them and still kept up the relationship now that he had moved on to another post. He was the obvious solution. In a letter, she tells him in full the story of the crisis, and begs him to come and take charge of Maurice in order that she may go with an easy mind. She knows that it means giving up a better post and she really cannot ask it; nevertheless, she does so; if he will sacrifice to their friendship two years of his life, she will promise him eternal gratitude. If he refuses, she cannot go at all and her husband will use his advantage freely. It is the kind of request that may succeed through sheer audacity and it succeeded on this occasion. Young Boucoiran took on a rôle which for many years afterwards he was never allowed to relinquish. A second letter to him is full of arrangements about money, routes, stopping places. Aurore refuses a request to meet him as they pass on their way to and from Paris. It would not be good policy for either of them.

Little Maurice was assured, when his mother went off, that she would be back within a week at the latest. How Boucoiran and the other members of the household dealt with this situation later is not recorded. Other letters to the tutor from Paris are a series of questions and instructions about the children, including Solange's medicine. He is to let her know at once if they are ill. The others would exaggerate in order to bring her back unnecessarily, and she is not coming for anything they may say.

George Sand's constant anxiety about her children and frequent minor sacrifices for them in the course of 'living her own life' make a tragi-comedy. It was a perpetual conflict – a perpetual endeavour to cover up the hard truth that she had, in fact, deserted them. A letter to Boucoiran a year or so later quotes a 'bitterly sour letter' from her brother. 'Your son is the best thing you ever produced; he loves you more than anybody in the world. Take care not to impair that feeling.' That, said the mother, could happen only if Maurice's heart was selfish and cold, and Boucoiran would save them from that.

And yet, it hardly pays for a sensitive person to be brutally selfish. It inflicts a kind of internal bruise, all the more injurious if it is unadmitted. Many of George Sand's later movements were obvious attempts to salve this intimate wound. It is another form of the almost inevitable dilemma of genius. George Sand had a genuine vocation, if anyone ever had, 'to live her own life,' and humanity would be the poorer in experience, if she had not done so. Even the immolated Boucoiran would never have been heard of, if he had not done something to make it easier for her.

Aurore Dudevant had something to go to in Paris.

Against her dreary existence at Nohant, had shone the gay Bohemian life of the young Parisians who came to La Châtre. It was a time of effervescence, political, social and literary. The second revolution had just been accomplished. Rousseau's ideas had come to their second flowering. The Saint-Simonites were advocating a very complete form of socialism and a feminist movement was beginning. In literature, Romanticism was in its most feverish phase. Eighteenth-century suavity and self-control were completely out of fashion; it was *de rigeur* to have violent emotions and to express them violently. Aurore and her friends were proud of styling themselves 'Hugolâtres.' Thus, in deserting the background of a provincial wife and mother, Aurore was not receding into isolation. The rebel background was ready for her. She had warm friendships among the young intellectuals who had come down to La Châtre, and, one of them, Jules Sandeau, was already, before she left Nohant, qualifying for the vacant position of 'He.'

Nevertheless, she began life in Paris alone. Hippolyte had been bullied into allowing her to use his apartment, and the young rebel set up there the desultory housekeeping that pleased her best. She revelled in her freedom. 'A sort of destiny drove me. I felt it invincible; and I threw myself into it resolutely; not a great destiny, I was too independent in my fancy to embrace any kind of ambition, but a destiny of moral liberty and poetic isolation, in a society from which I asked nothing but to forget me and let me earn my daily bread without slavery. . . . I had the ideal dwelling in the corners of my brain, and it needed only a few days of complete liberty to make it blossom. I carried it into the street, my feet on the cobbles, my shoulders covered with snow, my hands in my pockets, my stomach a little hollow sometimes, but my head full of dreams, melodies, colours, forms, rays and phantoms. I was no more a lady, nor yet was I a gentleman. People passed me on the pavement like a thing which might get in the way of busy folk passing. It was all one to me, me, who had no business. No one knew me, no one looked at me, no one addressed me; I was a lost atom in an immense crowd. No one said as at La Châtre, "There's Madame Aurore; she always wears the same hat and the same dress," nor, as at Nohant, "There's our lady posting on her big horse; she must be crazy to ride like that." In Paris, no one thought anything of me, no one saw me.'

She paid one or two formal visits of farewell to respectability. At the convent, the nuns had their own worries and paid her no attention. Her schooltime intimate friends, Jane and Aimée, did not know that they were seeing her for the last time, but she knew. 'What I was doing was very definite. I was openly shocking the rule of the world. I was consciously cutting myself off from it; and I must take it in good part that it should sever itself from me as soon as it saw my eccentricities.'

The particular eccentricity that stamped the future George Sand in the eyes of the public was, of course, her adoption of man's costume. People who receive great publicity are of two kinds, those who deliberately seek it and those who would shun it if they could. The latter are people who merely wish to go their own way. They are astounded, outraged, that other people cannot let them alone. They don't interfere, why should they be interfered with? They cannot realise that in going their own way they are, in fact, interfering – interfering with the unwritten social compact that one shall walk in the way of the herd. George Sand seems to have adopted her male costume simply for reasons of convenience – she had to tramp about Paris a great deal in her new way of life, she could not afford to go in a coach like a great lady; her skirts blew about, and became bedraggled; her feet ached in her thin shoes. Breeches and coat and boots were warm and comfortable and economical. A slim lad passed unnoticed where a woman could not. These are the reasons she herself gave, and they appear adequate. It seems better manners to accept a person's own explanation for her conduct, if it sufficiently explains it, as well as better science not to look for a complicated reason where a simple one will suffice. There are other indications, also, that George Sand had, in the first place, no cheap hankering for publicity. She did not use her own name for her novels, and evidently intended to remain anonymous until it became clear that that was impossible. When she wrote the *History of My Life*, apart from a few obscure allusions, she left out her love affairs.

But whether Aurore Dudevant welcomed it or not, publicity inevitably found out the one woman who was free of a lively set of young artists and writers who soon began to make themselves felt in the intellectual world; and the male costume inevitably became the symbol of revolt. The talent that was still necessary (for her allowance was quite inadequate) was quickly found. Association with Jules Sandeau naturally brought it to light; and introductions to editors and publishers came easily from her literary comrades. She was delighted to find that she could write. It was a possible future justification; and, sure of herself as she was, Aurore always craved external justification also. 'Indeed why should I bear them any grudge?' she wrote of the people who would condemn her. 'What could they know of my end, my future, my will? Did they know, did I myself know, if I had any talent, any perseverance? I had never told anyone the solution of the riddle of my thought; I had not yet proved it in any certain manner; and when I spoke of writing, it was with laughter and jest at the thing and at myself.'

Writing was for George Sand, in fact, always second and accessory to the business of living. This was one of the traits that most irritated her literary friends, especially in view of her immense success. Although she ultimately produced charming small-scale works of art when she came back to the peasant life that she knew, her talent was primarily journalistic. She was prolific – '*une vache à écrire,*' as an unkind critic put it. *Lélia* was written in six weeks. She made capital out of the ideas and movements of the time, and copy of herself and her friends, though she always denied actual portraiture. She exploited the romantic convention to its limits. Her more purely literary friends were, in turn, admiring, amused and annoyed. Success in popular journalism is always exasperating to struggling artists – that another should cheaply win the money and reputation which would be the saving of them, but which they cannot bring themselves to, or perhaps literally cannot, pay the price to obtain. George Sand never understood that, in becoming rich and famous, she was subtly insulting her artistic friends, and that her unbounded generosity with her winnings – she would always do anything for a friend, except, of course, own herself in the wrong – merely strained the spiritual situation still further.

At the moment, the business of living and the business of writing delightfully coincided. Very soon she and Jules Sandeau were both living together and collaborating in a novel. It was Aurore's first essay in her quest for the perfect mate, the second person in her trinity, and, of course, she thought that it would also be the final one.

Jules Sandeau, himself, gave a picture of Aurore at

this stage in a novel he wrote many years later. 'She had been brought up in the country and had now for the first time left it; and her manners showed a strange combination of boldness and timidity. Sometimes, indeed, she affected a kind of petulant brusquerie, the result of a secret uneasiness, and an ardour that ran to waste. She had almost a man's familiarity of address, so that it was easy to be intimate with her; but her haughty chastity and her instinctively aristocratic air mingled with her "abandon" certain suggestions, as it were, of a virgin, and of a duchess, contrasting strangely with her disdain for the proprieties and her ignorance of the world. All the evidence revealed in her a richly endowed nature, stirring impatiently beneath the weight of a wealth not yet called into activity. Life – palpitating life – seemed to move among the curls of her beautiful black hair; and there burnt as it were a hidden fire beneath her delicate and transparent skin. The purity of her brow indicated that the storms of passion had not yet broken upon that noble head; but the expression of her eyes, burning, yet weak and tired, spoke of terrible interior struggles, ceaseless but unavowed.'

George Sand inevitably acquired the reputation of a man-eater. 'Of those whom she has loved,' wrote de Musset's brother, 'all of them have left her hands more or less injured, disfigured and crippled for life.'

But there was clearly nothing of the Helen of Troy or of the Cleopatra in her. Her succession of distinguished lovers is not easily explained by ordinary standards. Not everyone even thought her good-looking. She had no superficial seductiveness. Balzac, one of her acquaintances who escaped the fascination, said that she had no coquetry and made a Frenchman's natural gallantry impossible; she was 'garçon, artiste, camarade,' but not seductive. She had immense vitality, but it was a vitality that seems to have expressed itself in lamentation rather than in gaiety. It seems probable that her preliminary attraction, what caused that riveting of the attention which is the first step to love, was, in fact, her singularity. Anything that excites attention, without being actually repulsive, is apt to arouse sex instinct – indeed, repulsion itself is not always a guarantee against it, to judge by the proposals to which people acquitted (however narrowly) of murder are notoriously subject. Once the attention was caught, George Sand's domination is easier to understand. Pagello, the least vocal of her lovers, has left the most vivid record of what it was like to fall in love with her.

'Passing beneath the windows of the Hôtel Danieli, I saw, on the first floor balcony, a young woman of somewhat melancholy countenance with very black hair and eyes of a decided and virile expression. Her attire had a certain singularity. Her hair was confined by a scarlet scarf, like a small turban. Round her neck she wore a cravat, daintily fastened to a collar white as snow; and she was smoking a long cigar with the assurance of a soldier, while she chatted with the fair-haired young man seated beside her.' He and his companion discussed her eagerly and wished they could make her acquaintance – an ambition which Pagello himself soon realised through his profession as a doctor. It developed into a friendship over the young man's sick-bed.

'You can imagine whether I was assiduous at the bedside of this patient. George Sand watched with me whole nights by his pillow. These watches were not silent, and the graces, the lofty spirit, the gentle trustfulness which she showed me drew me every day, every hour, and every minute nearer to her. We talked of literature, of Italian poets and artists. . . . At every turn of the conversation, she would interrupt to ask me what I was thinking about. I was confused, apologised profusely and blushed . . . then she would say with a slight smile and a subtle glance, "Ah, doctor, I bore you with my endless questions." . . . I cannot deny that the genius of this woman surprised and overwhelmed me.'

But when he received a fervid romantic love-letter from her, 'There were two contrary desires in me, one which panted ardently to see her, the other which would gladly have fled; but that one always lost . . . We went out together. When I felt myself in the open, I seemed to breathe more freely and spoke with greater ease and fluency. She told me . . . how many reasons she had to complain of Alfred de Musset . . . Then I saw my fate, I felt neither joy, nor distress, but I walked into it with my eyes shut.'

George Sand (the pen-name that she composed partly from that of her collaborator and first lover, soon became emphatically her own), so far from being the typical man-eater, had, in those early days, no notion how dangerous she was. And, even later, when the fact was forced upon her, she always regarded it with surprise and indignation. To herself, she was always the victim – the sport of other people's passions. Her ideas and desires seemed to her so right, so directly inspired by the God within her, that, if other people did not fall in with them, that was obviously their fault. She was so positive about it that those who were less certain in their views, constantly found themselves swept away by the force of her conviction. She was one of those persons to whom people find themselves apologising for the injuries she has done them.

Boucoiran, feeling, no doubt, that as deputy-mother, he had some standing in the matter, once ventured a protest against what he had heard of her way of living in

Paris. 'Your reproaches are very serious, my dear boy,' replied George Sand. 'Emanating from you, such reproaches constitute a grievance more serious still for me against you. You rebuke me on account of my numerous liaisons, my frivolous friendships. I never undertake to clear myself from imputations bearing on my character.' ... She has no great opinion of herself any more than of anyone else, she adds, and therefore leaves the field free to critics. But her friends must accept her whole and abjure any disapproval. 'When we discover great blots in the souls of those whom we love, we should carefully consider whether we ought to love them still in spite of the discovery. The most sensible course to pursue is to give them up; the most generous, to retain them. But, in order that our generosity should be delicate and complete, we must not tell them the truth, for that would be cruel.' Boucoiran subsided.

To Mme. d'Agoult she states her demands of a friend, when experience has taught her something of herself. 'Consider whether you can give your heart to a porcupine. I am capable of anything. I will play a thousand silly tricks. I will tread upon your toes; I will make rude replies without the least provocation; I will reproach you with a defect which you do not possess; I will suspect you of an intention which you never had; I will turn my back upon you; in short, I will make myself unbearable, until I am quite sure that I cannot make you cross and disgust you with me.' But if the aspiring friend can endure all this, she will then become her slave and humble admirer.

The one doubt that never seems to have crossed George Sand's mind was that the association was anything but supremely worth while for her friends and lovers, that the subordination of their own tastes and inclinations was anything but a reasonable demand in return for her affection. At first, they were apt to think so, too.

She demanded, in fact, an environment of saints. If it is a weakness of the saintly altruistic ideal that it implies egotism in others, it is a weakness in the more common egoistic ideal that it implies altruism in others. Jules Sandeau however, was no saint. And he was only twenty, seven years her junior. George Sand had kept her word and returned to Nohant and her rôle of mother for some months in 1832. She came back without warning, expecting to give her lover a joyful surprise, and found him in a compromising situation with a laundress.

It was the end of Jules Sandeau. She hustled him out without a moment's hesitation. For him, the momentary attraction of the laundress had meant nothing; and it was said that, to the end of his days, he could never hear George Sand's name mentioned without the tears coming into his eyes. But, for her, the outrage was absolute and final. She gave him money and sent him off to Italy on the instant, and then began to clear away every trace of him from her life. She has given notice for his apartment, she writes to his friend, Regnault, having paid the rent, she has taken away her own furniture and here are Jules' remaining effects for him to keep, since she will have nothing to do with him when he comes back. There will be no reunion; she is too deeply wounded to have any sentiment left for him but affectionate compassion. Since he must have lost his own respect, Regnault need not punish him by telling him that he has lost hers, unless he is foolish enough to make it necessary.

There followed one of the terrible spiritual slumps that always followed George Sand's phases of emotional exultation. Even her freedom seemed hardly worth having.

'This independence so dearly bought, it is necessary to know how to enjoy and I am no longer capable of that. My heart has aged twenty years and nothing in life smiles at me any longer. There are no more deep passions or lively joys for me. All is said.'

Sainte-Beuve, whom George Sand had cast, as she cast all her friends for specific parts in her drama, for the rôle of Father Confessor, was much concerned about her state. He advised fresh society and new friendships, and sent to her everyone who he thought might interest her. The malicious story that he 'gave her Mérimée' as a consolation, and that she wrote the next day and reproached him for his present has this much basis. George Sand could not do without the second person of her trinity and a belief in the essential rightness of one's impulses does not develop the habit of patience. Mérimée seemed a possibility on the face of him and a furiously creative imagination did the rest. He had carried Solange, who intermittently stayed with her mother at this time, on his shoulder, when she fell asleep at the Opera. His cynical nonchalance was therefore strength of character, concealing a deep tenderness. Thus she met, as she told Sainte-Beuve, 'a man without hesitations, calm and strong, who understood nothing of my nature and laughed at my troubles. The strength of his mind fascinated me completely; for eight days, I thought he had the secret of happiness which he would teach to me, that his contemptuous carelessness would heal me of my childish susceptibilities. I thought that he had suffered like me and that he had conquered his external sensibility....'

'I imagined that a fascination which had lasted only a few days might decide the course of my life. And, in the end, I behaved at thirty as a girl of fifteen would never have behaved.' ... But she is not, of course, to blame for that. 'Why should I be ashamed to be ridiculous, if I have not been guilty?'

Mérimée, as he made clear later in *La Double Méprise*, had entered upon the liaison in a very different spirit. It was not an aspiration of the soul to him – merely a pleasant episode in the 'comedy of love.' He believed in taking love lightly, and George Sand's grimness over it quickly alarmed him. Her necessity for sentimental analysis shocked him, as it sometimes shocked other men. *C'est une femme débauchée à froid par curiosité*, he said later, *plus que par tempérament*. In other words, this mental habit of classifying and labelling states of soul, as they come and go, fostered in those days by the fashionable romanticism, is both a stimulant to, and a drag on, emotion. Emotions expressed take on a stronger reality; emotions analysed are apt to lose their *élan*. The self-consciousness of George Sand's love disgusted Mérimée. This divergence in attitude is sometimes taken to be a natural sex difference; in any case, it emerged here in its extreme form. Mérimée wanted his love-affairs light and gay, but he also wanted them spontaneous. Impulse on principle did not appeal to him. The shock to George Sand was equally great. 'The experience failed completely. I wept with suffering, disgust and discouragement. Instead of finding a love able to pity and compensate me, I found only a bitter and frivolous raillery. That was all.'

The two separated, mortal enemies, after a week. The cynical lover was of no more use than the unfaithful one.

George Sand's next essay was with a much younger man. In some respects, he was a highly experienced and sophisticated young man – he already considered himself burnt out at twenty-two in the true Byronic style. His own account shows that, with others of his contemporaries, he regarded himself as belonging to what corresponded to our post-war generation. The earthquake of the Revolution and the Napoleonic wars, on this theory, had left a youth drained of hope, of idealism, of the springs of action. Alfred de Musset was, however, a poet, unmistakeably a poet from birth like Chatterton or Keats; and poets are people who can never rely upon their own sophistication. He began to play with George Sand on the ruins of his spoilt young life – the game of literary congeniality, exchange of poems and books, mutual confidences, Bohemian 'rags,' the high-spirited clowning of the essentially melancholy. 'You know me well enough,' he wrote to her, 'to know that never the ridiculous word "will you? or won't you?" will issue from my lips. There is the Baltic sea between you and me in this respect. You can give only moral love – and I can return it to no one . . . but I can be, if you think me worthy – not even your friend – that is too moral for me – but a sort of casual and unexacting comrade without jealousy or quarrel, capable of smoking tobacco, playing the fool in your peignoirs, and catching colds in the head philosophising with you under all the chestnut trees in Europe.'

Either of the two would probably have been clever enough to know in anyone else's case how this talk of not being in love would end; but they transparently thought themselves safe, and very soon after, followed de Musset's inevitable avowal that he was in love with her. 'I have been so ever since the first day I came to your house.' George Sand, on her side, had seen him as a lost lamb to be mothered and brought back to the fold, a brilliant young genius to be reclaimed before it was too late; it is an idea that develops quickly into an all-absorbing mission.

'I have fallen in love with Alfred de Musset,' she wrote to Sainte-Beuve. 'It is not a caprice this time but a true attachment, which I will explain in full in another letter. I cannot undertake to promise for this affection a duration which would make it appear to you as sacred as the affections to which you are susceptible. I once loved for six years, and another time for three, and this time I do not really know how long it is likely to last.' It is a new kind of love – 'both the love of a young man and the friendship of a comrade.' At first, she had repulsed it, but has now yielded and is happy.

Her object in writing, she says, is to contradict a scandal. People have said that Planche (a well-known literary critic) was her lover; this is absolutely untrue. 'It is now very important to me that people should know that he is not. Although it is quite indifferent to me if they think he has been.

'You will understand that I cannot have any suspicions that I would be on the same terms with two men at once; that would not suit any of us three.'

It was a point of morality with which the God within her had never yet come into conflict. But the God within one is an erratic God.

There have been endless explanations of the failure of the love-affair of George Sand and Alfred de Musset. No explanation is really necessary. It is more remarkable that, with all the quirks of human nature and all the tricks of circumstance, an intimate human relationship ever can be harmonious. In artists, who are, in a sense, more human than humanity, the likelihood is still further diminished. It would have been a miracle if it had been a success.

The outline of the affair is well-known. The two lovers set off to Italy, partly in the spirit of adventure, partly, no doubt, to escape their notoriety. Practical matters were settled with the despatch and absoluteness with which George Sand always swept such cobwebs away when her mind was set upon anything. Solange was sent back to Nohant. Maurice, now at a Lycée in Paris, and very dependent on his mother's visits, was told by letter that she was going away for her rheumatism and exhorted to write often. Boucoiran had the job of closing the flat, collecting money due to her and forwarding remittances.

'Good-bye, my dear friend,' she wrote to him, 'I especially request you to give me news of my boy, and to fill my place towards him. I really do not know how I could manage my life, if I had not your kind friendship and everlasting kindness to help and comfort me.'

Alfred de Musset's mother, who broke at this point the convention that a young Frenchman's parents should ignore his extra-matrimonial *affaires*, describes how her opposition was overwhelmed.

'At nine o'clock in the evening, I was informed that someone was asking for me downstairs; I went down, followed by a servant, with no idea what was coming. I entered the carriage, seeing a woman there by herself. It was she. Then she used all the eloquence she was mistress of to persuade me to trust my son to her, declaring that she would love him as a mother, that she would look after him better than I could myself. What can I say? The siren tore my consent from me. I gave in, all in tears and against my heart.'

In Italy, friction soon developed. Literary jealousy, George Sand's reckless conversation, her trick of prevarication (probably the legacy of her years as a dutiful wife), Alfred de Musset's moodiness and profligate habits have all been offered as the source of the trouble. Partly it seems to have been the same difficulty as with Mérimée.

Alfred de Musset, with his youthful high-spirits, and flashing intuitions deeper than anything George Sand ever knew, could not live in the intense atmosphere that she created; and he was too young and too spoilt to have learnt self-restraint in expressing his discomfort. George Sand's subsequent letters show that it was what he said rather than what he did that had cut deepest. No one – man or woman – could perhaps forgive being told that she looked like 'a sick bird,' even without the fatal 'You bore me.' Infidelities are small things compared to those. The allusion recurs even in the most friendly and forgiving letters she afterwards wrote to him.

The climax came with the cool announcement one day in Venice, 'George, I was mistaken, I beg your pardon, but I do not love you.' A letter she wrote to him later goes over the unhappy story. She would have gone then, she said, but she was hardly recovered from an illness: Alfred had no money, and she did not know if he would accept it from her. She could not leave him alone in a foreign country, penniless and not knowing the language. They tried to take up their life again as comrades. George, however, felt herself released; her self-respect and her insulted femininity demanded instant compensation; and, with her, to want a thing was to go and get it. When de Musset fell seriously ill, she called in the young doctor Pagello, who had observed her on the balcony.

The love-affair that developed over Alfred de Musset's sick-bed was the crux of the drama that produced so great a sensation and so many works of literature – George Sand's *Elle et Lui* and *Intimate Journal*, Alfred de Musset's *Confession d'un Enfant du Siècle* and *Nuit d'Octobre*, Paul de Musset's *Lui et Elle*, besides endless versions and commentaries by outsiders.

George Sand, as always, felt herself intimately right.

Alfred had disowned her; she needed a quiet, unexacting, supporting love. The maternal love had failed her; so she cast Pagello for a fatherly lover, and for some time he was hypnotised into fulfilling the part. Alfred became their poor, sick, erring child. Alfred, himself, weak, overwhelmed, in the hands of his nurse and his doctor, dropped into his part like the boy he still remained in many respects. He accepted George's version. He deserved nothing, but these two magnanimous grown-ups had forgiven him and felt only kindness and solicitude for him. His love for George revived, when he found that he had been superseded, but it was a love attenuated by physical weakness. Nevertheless, as he became stronger, he could not endure the situation as it was. George saw no reason why they should not all go on living together happily, but Alfred felt that he must go. He left, amid tears and solicitude, and made his slow way back to France over the Alps, followed by anxious and affectionate letters.

The drama was kept up by correspondence for some time. Even Pagello and de Musset were induced to exchange stilted little notes in their respective characters. But it is dangerous to design a drama in real life in which someone else is cast for the self-abnegating part. Alfred found in Paris that the story had preceded him, and that other people did not see it in the heroic light in which it had appeared in those last days at Venice. His friends were furious. To them, it was obvious that George Sand had casually thrown him over, in her usual way, for a later fancy. Alfred himself soon became uncertain how to think about it. Egotism pulls both ways in such matters. If the ex-lover takes the blame for the rupture, he at once makes himself responsible for a brutal destruction, and, if he has any regrets, exposes himself to his own remorse. If he puts the blame on the other side, he has the humiliating rôle of having been jilted. George Sand preferred the second alternative in this dilemma (the point is worked out in *Elle et Lui*), for to be guilty in her own eyes was to her the one impossible catastrophe. Alfred de Musset could not decide which to choose. Sometimes he saw George still as a martyred guardian angel; sometimes, as a vampire. And, deeper still, was the poet's intuition that such appearances are shams, that the reality is something more subtle and not an occasion for cheap distribution of praise or blame. In *Confession d'un Enfant du Siècle*, he takes most of the blame himself, in fact, re-enacts the drama that George Sand had designed in Venice; Paul de Musset's *Lui et Elle*, claimed to be based on his brother's confidences, gives the rôles of victim and villain ferociously reversed. But *Nuit d'Octobre* is the poet's version. The dialogue with his muse presents the conflict in action, and shadows the transcendental solution.

'If I must still speak of my suffering, I know not what name it should bear, whether it was love, madness, pride, experience, nor if anyone in the world might profit by it.'

When George Sand wrote her version many years later, after Alfred's death, Buloz the publisher rejected the first draft. Of course, he says diplomatically, he knows that it is nothing but the bare truth. But it might appear more convincing if she tried to write as if Alfred de Musset were there to contradict her.

Meanwhile, the connection had not been severed. And the correspondence shows that it could not be, because neither of the two desired it. They were still lovers – lovers who had outraged each other mortally, but had placed too high a stake in each other to be able to abandon it. The little drama had this at its root. They tried desperately for a new adjustment. They were comrades, brothers, or mother and son, they told themselves, and their physical union had been a kind of spiritual incest. But when George came back to Paris, bringing Pagello, who had abandoned his practice and prospects to go with her, a passion that was now partly hatred blew the fiction to pieces. George was shocked and bewildered to find how Alfred's attitude had changed from the humble acceptance of Venice. 'So many people come between us that you are not allowed to stop brooding over the "injury" I have done you. . . . Poor Alfred ! If no one knew, you would forgive me.'

For it quickly became a question of Alfred's forgiveness. From being the martyr, George Sand found herself cast for the murderer's part. She was outraged. But she was also desperately in love with Alfred again. Pagello had not lasted well; he, in his turn, became jealous; and he was out of place and uncomfortable among the young Bohemians of Paris. 'Is elevated and trustful love possible ?' she confides to Alfred about him. 'Must I not die without finding it ? Always seizing phantoms and pursuing shadows ! I am tired of it. Yet I loved this generous man sincerely and seriously, this man as romantic as myself and whom I thought stronger than I. I loved him as a father and you were the child of both. Now he has become a feeble creature, suspicious, unjust, making German quarrels.' The disgraced Pagello was left in Paris for Boucoiran to look after, while George went to Nohant for the children's holidays, and he was finally shipped back to Italy by that loyal aide-de-camp.

When George came back from Nohant, the desperate situation renewed itself. She and Alfred could neither live together, nor apart. He could not forget or forgive the Venetian episode; and inflicted on her all the ingenious tortures of jealous love, with all the resources of a poet,

– furies, coldnesses, insults, and then helpless appeals. For once in her life, George Sand wavered; she was almost harried into accepting the blame, after all. In her *Intimate Journal*, which seems to have been in the nature of letters never posted, she does intermittently accept it. 'You say "one cannot love two men at the same time." Nevertheless, that was what happened to me. It happened once, but it will not happen again. You are crazy when you say "She will do it to-morrow, because she did it yesterday!" You ought to say just the opposite. Am I stupid or insensitive? Do I not suffer from my follies and mistakes? Are lessons of no value to women like me? . . . One may commit a crime unconsciously. Whether an action is praised as holy or condemned as horrible is often determined by the after effect, or it may be decided by chance . . . That Italian! God knows why his first word did not draw from me a cry of horror! And why did I yield, why, why? Do I know? I know that you have broken me because of him, and that for my involuntary crime you have punished me as human judges punish only the deliberate assassin.'

She will regain his respect by six months' decent living with the companionship of distinguished and high-minded men. She must make herself a dignified past. . . . Let him go to another woman who may teach him to believe in love. 'I, alas, have only taught him to deny love. Mea Culpa! Alfred, I am going to write a book. You will see that my soul is not vindictive, for this book will be a terrific accusation against myself.'

But how can a person to whom impulse is sacred own herself in the wrong? Whether, if she had done so, it would have pacified de Musset seems doubtful. But, in the letters she actually sent to him, she still told him that her relations with Pagello were no business of his. How could the man who had called her 'Boredom personified, dreamer, stupid, *réligieuse*' have a right to ask anything about her relations with another man? And he has no more right now '*à présent que je redeviens ta maîtresse*' than he had then.

The logic was unanswerable. But what shocked Alfred and their audience was not that she had acted independently on her impulse, but that she could have had such an impulse at such a moment. What was infinitely worse it shocked George Sand herself. Constancy is as much a natural desire of developed humanity as the impulse of passion itself – less violent at the moment, but more enduring. And to the person to whom impulse is law, conflicting desires create the worst of hells. It seems to have been this inadmissible question – was I right or wrong? – that demoralised George Sand, even more than de Musset's sadistic tyrannies.

The affair dragged on its tragic course half publicly through the winter of 1834-5, with endless recrimination, daily final partings, suggestions of suicide and murder and passionate reunions. Paris watched it breathlessly. 'Ah! she really appears quite decent in spite of everything,' George heard an old lady remark at the Opera. Sainte-Beuve was involved again. He was asked to meet George to discuss a question of life and death at the Collège Henri Quatre, since they could not talk alone at her flat. Afterwards, he sent a note to de Musset imploring him not to admit her if she came again. It would do them both too much harm. George's last letter, which begins '*Non, non c'est assez!*' resumes her own rôle. She has loved him like a mother, but she cannot save him. She would become evil if she stayed with him, for she cannot fight him as he says she should. 'I don't know how to struggle.' God has made her gentle, yet proud.

'My God, what sort of life am I leaving you to? Drunkenness, wine, women, still and always.' But she can do nothing, so why prolong her shame and his torment? The more he loses the right to be jealous, the more he becomes so. It is like a judgment of God on him. But she has still her own children.

It was over at last. And never again does George Sand appear to have questioned her own rightness in the matter.

In this way ended, in mutual exhaustion, the most tempestuous episode of George Sand's tempestuous life. And it was followed by the worst moral and nervous slump that she ever experienced. Her letters and conversation were suicidal. She even doubted her gospel. 'It may be that I have wearied the heart and abused the mind by an adventurous life and false ideas; but I am dying of it, do you see, and for those who love me it is only a question of guiding me gently to my tomb. Tell me what is this that has been happening in me these ten years and more; this disgust of everything, this devouring *ennui*, which follows my most vivid enjoyments, and which more and more grows upon and crushes me; is it a sickness of my brain or a consequence of my destiny? Am I terribly right in hating life? Am I criminally wrong in not accepting it?' She must be a freak, she thinks, not to feel the love of life as others do. She is ashamed that she cannot put an end to it; she sometimes thinks herself so used up by work, love and grief that she is good for nothing more; and then suddenly sees that she is going to die in all the force of her physical strength and the power of her soul.

An entry in her Journal, some time later, prescribes the best method for dealing with such states of mind. Don't bother about original causes, but save your strength to fight the effects. Observe what brings on the crises and avoid it. When you are normal, remember that the

PL

delirium will come again, and when it is upon you, remember that it will end. Eat little and often. Don't weep; don't nourish anger and vengeance. Tears and anger produce more tears and anger.

She recovered, of course. Such temperaments cannot keep even their griefs for long. And she still sought the ideal, but with less hope and greater readiness to accept obvious substitutes. If their love-affair smashed de Musset, it coarsened George Sand. Which is the greater penalty is a matter of taste.

The framework of her domestic life, to which she had always kept open the retreat, carried George Sand through the next year. There were her children. There was Nohant and her friends there, especially Rollinat, the magistrate, whom she regarded as her *alter ego*, her male counterpart, not her complement. They understood each other; and took gloomy walks together, sometimes silent, sometimes pouring out confidences, but never making the mistake of trying to comfort each other. Then there was her work; the necessary practical basis for everything else. In Venice, she had produced a novel and a book of travels, and she must always go on writing. Complete personal liberty, unsupported by a very large income, means economic slavery. George Sand averaged two books a year for fifty years. She worked at least seven or eight hours a day, often more. It was one of the things that had depressed de Musset. And she supported upon the proceeds everyone who came along – lovers, friends, family and dependents.

But the de Musset affair had not only coarsened, it had frightened her. It had been so public, and public opinion was against her. There are impulses of fear as well as of desire; and even the most independent souls are not immune from them. The fear of loneliness, for instance, had always been strong in George Sand. After the Sandeau episode, she had written, 'Growing old matters little to me, but it matters much that I should not grow old in solitude.' This dread, as much as passion or idealism, had accounted for Mérimée and for Pagello. Then there were the allied social fears – the fear of ridicule and the fear of outlawry. The approval, or, at least, the tolerance, of his kind is almost as important to that inescapably social animal, man, as the satisfaction of hunger or sex. The de Musset affair had temporarily made George Sand something of an outlaw even among her own rebel set, and she was not always fanatic enough to invert, and make a glory of, her punishment. She cared enough for her children to see them sometimes as her hostages to society. Shall she, she asks Rollinat, bring them up to follow her? Even if she tries, they cannot escape contrary influences; moreover, they inevitably see for themselves her sufferings in the eternal struggle, 'her ulcerated heart, her knees broken at every step on the obstacles of real life?' She fears that if she taught them to follow her, they would come back later to reproach her. Letters to Maurice a little later show the see-saw of her dilemma. They are full of socialistic sentiment; they tell him to take no notice of what he is taught by his history professors. But outwardly he is to conform. He is to show her letters to no one, and to keep their contents secret.

Some new adjustment became vitally necessary. As she recovered from her depression, there arose a new need – an intellectual need to understand and universalise her experience – a sense that even a rebel may require the principles and standards which give a kind of alternative respectability. In this expanding and receptive phase, George Sand met a man of powerful intellect, overwhelming eloquence and schoolmaster's temperament.

The encounter had the necessary touch of drama. She was more at Nohant now and the children were growing up. They brought about the second big domestic explosion. Maurice, ordered by his father to fetch some cream, went and sat by his mother instead. Dudevant's always simmering rage broke out. He tried to turn out both mother and son, fetched his gun, and threatened to strike her. George Sand was not sufficiently frightened to put up with this. She decided to fight and to be rid of him finally at any price. The law-suit was a provincial sensation in the summer of 1836. Dudevant seems to have been ill-advised in basing his case upon the ancient Aurélien de Sèze espisode. Aurélien behaved perfectly and gave George Sand all possible support. Their platonic letters were read in court in all their high-minded austerity. Dudevant's own infidelities were only too easily proved. And George Sand had the assistance of Michel de Bourges, a brilliant lawyer and socialist agitator. Dudevant found himself once again outclassed and made his final submission. He abandoned the case for a compromise that gave George almost all that she had wanted – the children, Nohant and half the family income. She was at last undisputed mistress of her little kingdom.

Preparations for the trial had naturally thrown her much into contact with Michel de Bourges. He was not an outwardly prepossessing person, but, when she went over with a friend to see him at Bourges, he talked to them until the small hours, and the two parties saw each other home nine times. George and her friend Fleury had nightmare after it, and, though she wanted to stay and see Michel again the next day, Fleury was terrified and they fled away to Nohant, to the lecturer's great offence.

He forgave her, however, and, after the trial was safely over, succeeded to the position of 'Lui.' 'Everard,' as she called him, alone among George Sand's lovers and friends had thus the opportunity of grafting upon her settled principles; but he missed it. Or perhaps it was, after all, a hopeless enterprise from the outset. Her writings and activities, however, took on a more definitely socialistic tone from this time forward. But she still fought shy of committing herself. When the Saint-Simonites invited her to become the High Priestess in their new religion, which included socialism and free love, and waited on her with gifts and garlands, she told them that she was a soldier, not a priest. Her job was to clear the ground for them as regenerators. 'I am not one of those strong and vigorous minds which can bind themselves by oath to a new path.' In *Letters to Marcia* which she wrote for Abbé de Lammenais of the *Monde* her pen ran away with her on the subject of women's wrongs. The Abbé could not go so far. She did not know her real opinions, George Sand wrote to him, but was driven by inspiration 'which may be the voice of Truth or may be only the impertinent voice of pride.' But she made it clear that she intended to bank on the former alternative. The series had to be given up.

Meanwhile, 'Everard' failed, because his ideas of universal liberty did not include that of individual liberty – at least, for his disciples. He was jealous and possessive. One had either to submit or fight, said George Sand, and she passed three years doing alternatively one or the other. He expected a woman to devote herself to him heart and soul. She must prostrate herself before him and say to him, 'You are great, sublime, incomparable. You are more perfect than God. Your face radiates light; where your feet have trod nectar is distilled; you have nothing remotely resembling a fault and you have all conceivable virtues.'

George Sand had begun by accepting this rôle, but it requires more than an intellectual infatuation to support such a strain for long. And, no doubt, her position at Nohant was acting as a restorative. There can be few better tonics for damaged self-confidence than to be a feudal landlord on a country estate. There were agonies and depressions over the affair, but no such moral débâcle as those over Sandeau and de Musset. Everard was naturally outraged when his worshipper began to stand up and look critical. But George Sand soon ceased to care. 'No letter from Everard to-day,' says an entry in her Journal. 'He is angry again. Happy man, to find anything worth getting angry about !' By July, 1836, she had had enough of him. 'I am sick and tired of great men. I should like to see them all in Plutarch. . . . Let great men be carved in marble or cast in bronze and no more said about them. . . . They are worse to their friends than to their enemies.' So the pedagogue lover went the way of the others.

Sairte-Beuve, the Father Confessor, was disowned about the same time. 'I cannot understand Sainte-Beuve,' she wrote, 'I have loved him *paternally*. He devoted his life to vex me, to grumble at me, to pry into my actions and to suspect me; so much so that I at last sent him to the devil.'

At Nohant, she sometimes felt the misgivings inevitable to the sensitive person who has at last ensured that she shall always get her own way. Is she becoming a tyrant to her children and household ? the Journal asks. 'Not a hair in your dominion dares to rise against you. At the breath of your anger those who are near you tremble like leaves in the wind of a storm. Unfortunate one ! the fear you inspire only increases your loneliness.' Then she resumes herself. 'You see now that you have done no wrong. Your heart is good and your conscience does not trouble you. Then why all this suffering?'

Several shadowy Prince Consorts succeeded 'Everard;' Malefille, Maurice's new tutor, a mild nonentity, Pierre Leroux, a gentle, absent-minded social theorist, who came and went easily; and perhaps others.

But in 1838 George Sand again met an equal, or superior, and desire and fear arose and fought their battle again. The affair with Chopin began with hesitations. George Sand wanted it to remain an ideal, or, at least, a very occasional, love. She was full of scruples – Chopin's health, his entanglement with Marie Wodenska. 'I do not want to be forced into the position of bad angel.' She will only take him, if it may be regarded as a rescue. She herself is unwilling to abandon herself to passion, in spite of the furnace still smouldering in her heart. There is the welfare of her children. Also, there is someone with whom she can never break (Malefille), 'the only man who has been my lover for a year without causing me any suffering.' She cannot undertake Chopin's whole existence. She feels that their love must be in heavenly snatches like their first kiss. . . . It would be best if he, like her, were capable of a soul love and a body love. They would share occasional beautiful days, but not the sordidness of life. She has nevertheless no theories about possession or restraint. 'I have trusted implicitly to my instincts, which are always noble. I have sometimes made mistakes about other people, but never about myself. . . . Above all, I believe in fidelity. . . . People have failed in fidelity to me, and I myself have failed in it. And yet I have never felt remorse because I always discerned a sort of fatality in my own infidelities; an instinct of straining up to the ideal, which urged me to leave the imperfect and pursue my search for perfection.'

This analysis is in a letter to Chopin's intimate friend, Count Albert Grzymala, and it concludes with an invitation to Nohant, including Chopin if he wishes to come. But she must know in good time, so that she can send Malefille to Paris. It will be easy to find a pretext, and he is quite unsuspicious.

In the outcome, George Sand and Chopin shared the sordidness of life for eight years. Its sordidness was increased by the fact that Chopin was a consumptive, and needed frequent nursing. The records that remain represent it as a maternal slavery on George Sand's part and very little else. But then these records are principally her own accounts written after the final rupture; and the account of one of the interested parties in a love-affair after it has come to a disastrous end, is not evidence; still less, if the person in question suffers from an intimate necessity for being always in the right. Chopin, on his side, rarely expressed himself in words. The terrible night in Majorca when he thought that George and Maurice were drowned in the floods and greeted them as a spectre greeting spectres, 'Ah, yes, I knew that you were dead,' appears in his records as the sixth Prelude in B Minor. His comments on the final rupture are probably in similar form for those who can interpret them. But almost his only verbal comment was a lament for his eight years of a *vie rangée*.

In spite of George Sand's insistence on its inconveniences, the liaison seems to have become, in fact, a liaison of convenience on both sides, as soon as its initial impulse was worn out. Chopin needed a home; his life as a solitary adventuring artist in Paris was killing him; and, assisted by a visit to England, did indeed kill him very

quickly after he left Nohant. George Sand needed a
'Lui,' and, by this time, stability had begun to seem an
important element in the relationship, even at the price of
romance. She had intended, according to her own
account, not to continue the affair after the winter in
Majorca. It was to have been a honeymoon and no more.
But when they were all in Paris afterwards, Chopin living
in his own flat, he would come round with a twisted face
and an extinguished voice every day and tell her how
marvellously well he was. She describes how she thought
the matter out very plainly; whether it appeared actually
so clear-cut at the time seems doubtful. It was a question
of conscience, she says. Her main object was to arrange
her life as best possible for her children. Could she accept
Chopin, too ? 'I was under no illusion of passion.' She
had only a sort of maternal adoration for the artist. She
reflected, too, that she might still be young enough to
have a genuine passion; and she was determined never to
submit to an influence which might distract her from her
children. But she decided that this 'gentle friendship'
might, on the other hand, help to protect her from it.

Chopin's presence, in short, was an insurance against
the passionate storms which she had learnt to dread. He
was temperamental and difficult in his way; but he was
nevertheless a gentle soul. He could be brilliant and witty
in a small company, and he was always distinguished. He
gave the household at Nohant a tone that it had lacked.
When George Sand referred to him as the 'host' of her
establishment during these years, she was not merely being
euphemistic. He respected her and called her 'his angel';
and it was an impudent pupil who added that she was an
angel with very large wings which sometimes knocked
against you and hurt you. They had no quarrels until
the final one.

It seemed that in this 'second-best' love to which she had resigned herself at last, George Sand's life might go on, indefinitely, in a peaceful Indian summer. But other people's, younger people's, desires, had not outgrown their turbulent phase. George Sand's children, like herself, had had a confused upbringing, and one that hardly made for stable standards or consideration for other people's difficulties. Like their mother, they thought that impulses were there to be gratified. With Maurice, her son, George Sand sympathised. She regarded him as peculiarly her child, the extension of her own existence. 'My son was myself,' she told Flaubert, 'therefore much more woman than my daughter, who was an imperfect man.' Accordingly, there was the same sacredness about Maurice's desires as there had been about his mother's. He grew up an artistic dilettante – writer, artist, collector, dabbler in science, very expensive, but never grudged anything he wanted.

Solange was a different matter. She had always been difficult. Her impulses frequently conflicted with her mother's. 'Nothing has ever affected her,' wrote George Sand of her severely. 'She has always done whatever she wished.' She rejoiced after the passage to Majorca, that her ten-year-old daughter had 'lost most of her venom in sea-sickness.' Some twelve years later, the same daughter was writing to her, '*Jeunesse oblige*. . . . It is absolutely necessary that one should be happy when one is young. When *is* one to be happy, if not then? Happiness! I regard it as the most sacred right of youth. Duty? It is a fine word that means nothing. Virtue? It is a deception.'

It seems a piece of poetic justice, such as is rarely found in real life, that George Sand's last love-affair should have been wrecked over her daughter's first. The situation had gradually become strained at Nohant, as the children grew older. Solange, in spite of her 'venom,' was a favourite with the gentle Chopin. But Solange always quarrelled with Maurice. The household began to split on lines very much the same as those on which normal households frequently split – father and daughter against mother and son.

George Sand had imported into Nohant, Augustine, her niece, on her mother's side, a girl who was definitely 'of the people.' Whether or not the scandal which made her Maurice's mistress was true, Solange bitterly resented her presence, and Chopin shared her dislike. George Sand tried the same remedy as her own perplexed relations had tried in her own case. She got Solange engaged at eighteen to a neighbouring squire. It went so far that the bridal party, including Chopin, reached Paris; and then, at the last moment, Solange refused to sign the contract. Her elopement with a penniless young sculptor followed almost at once. George Sand disapproved of him on the score of his past; but, when a hasty marriage became necessary, she made up her mind to make the best of it. A month later, the young husband was threatening Maurice with a hammer. George Sand intervened, and got hit. 'That diabolical pair went off yesterday, head over ears in debt,' she wrote to a friend. 'My God! I had done nothing to deserve such a daughter!'

Chopin was away in Paris at the time. Solange, starving with her husband, appealed to him, and he came to her help. And so he, too, was told that he might not come back to Nohant, until he had disowned Solange, since it seemed that he loved the daughter better than the mother.

George Sand and Chopin met once or twice later and exchanged a few words. He was said to have been the first to tell her that she had become a grandmother. But, when he died, about a year later, his friends refused to admit her to his death bed.

The final loneliness that she had feared was upon George Sand; but not until the acuteness of the fear had already gone. 'The gravest and most grievous phase of my life,' she called it, but she was conscious of her entrenchment at Nohant. She could philosophise about it calmly, if sadly. 'My child,' she wrote to the young friend who had remarked on the bruising capacity of her wings, 'life is just a bitter irony, and those who are such fools as to love and trust will eventually end their careers in gloomy laughter and heart-broken sobs, as I hope will soon be my lot.'

Before Chopin was dead, she was taking a leading part in the Revolution of 1848 and writing, 'I live, I am strong, I am active, I am twenty years old.'

There was no longer a 'Lui,' but the urgent need for him was past. At forty-five, George Sand passed easily into a matriarchal phase. It was suggested later, that Manceau, an obscure engraver who lived at Nohant and acted as a general steward and secretary, was her lover, but if so, he was merely another vague Prince Consort, a privileged member of the small court with which she surrounded herself. George Sand had no occasion to fear actual desertion, for she had Nohant, she had money, and she had enormous and ever-increasing literary prestige. Her son was absolutely dependent upon her, materially and spiritually. He wandered away now and then for short periods, but always came back. He married late, a gentle and quiet young friend of the family, the daughter of the man who 'sat' for the hero of George Sand's *The Master Mosaic-Workers*. The couple were always content to live at Nohant, where George Sand even made the retiring Lena play hostess sometimes. Their children were born and brought up there, and were the delight of their grandmother's old age.

There were also temporary reconciliations with Solange, who, after her separation from her husband, was advised by her mother that she must now be content to live in quiet, simple retirement, and might find that she could write. But Solange could never stay at Nohant for any length of time, and after her little daughter died, her vitality refused to be damped down any longer. In the end, her career became superficially like that of her mother, with the vital difference that, so far from her supporting her lovers, they were her only means of support.

After the tempestuous events of the forties, George Sand lived another twenty odd years. She did some of her best work in the time – the delightful idylls of country life so remote from the lurid romanticism of *Indiana* and *Lélia*. There was a private theatre at Nohant, where she and Maurice amused themselves in dramatic experiment. There were frequent comings and goings to and from Paris. There was a constant stream of visitors, often men and women of distinction. There were domestic events, Augustine's marriage, Maurice's, Manceau's death, the birth of the grandchildren and the cares and pleasures of their upbringing. George Sand took an interest in everyone who presented himself. A young poet, disconcerted by her prolonged gaze, was told, 'I contemplate you as an undiscovered country.' Amic, writing to her at twenty for advice on his love affairs, was told to keep himself innocent and marry early for love, and, when he wanted to know what she thought of his comedy, was invited to stay at Nohant and read it to her. 'She never left a letter unanswered,' said her secretary. It is not, in the aggregate, a small credit to put into the balance against the sufferings of those who once knew her too well.

Her own later letters speak much of the happiness of living in the lives of others and claim a serene detachment. She no longer, she told Flaubert, demanded reciprocity from the people she loved. She could admire them as she admired pictures and statues, 'for what they are in themselves.' Sometimes old tragedies returned, as in the terrible sentence 'my heart is a cemetery,' which Jules Sandeau capped with his 'a necropolis, rather.' And there is an occasional spurt of her old exigence in her letters to Flaubert, the chosen friend of her old age, who enjoyed their half-playful correspondence, but dreaded coming to Nohant. 'I, who have not buried myself alive in literature,' she tells him a little sharply, 'have laughed and lived a great deal during these holidays.' She was always trying to draw him out, this patient artist who needed a triple protective shell for his delicate work; but it was no tragedy when she did not succeed. And she was too old, and perhaps, to the creator of Madame Bovary, too unconsciously comic, for him to resent her, as the artist lovers of her youth had sometimes resented her.

'She saved herself, others she could not save,' says one critic. If to grow old with dignity and quiet happiness, is to save oneself, George Sand certainly achieved it. By surviving the age of strong impulse, she came to have no impulses that she could not gratify. She had, of course, exceptional luck; or, perhaps it is fairer to say, the talent to wrest justification of her way of life. Hers was hardly the programme that would have made serenity and happiness possible in an old age of obscure poverty. But, as matriarch of Nohant, she attained it. 'I am still on my feet,' she wrote at the age of sixty-six. 'No old age yet or rather normal old age, the calmness of *virtue*, that thing that people ridicule and that I mention in mockery, but that corresponds by an emphatic and silly word to a condition of forced inoffensiveness, without merit in consequence, but agreeable and good to experience.'

The people she had overturned in her first tempestuous rush had not, after all, suffered for nothing. She had been a pioneer and, in these quiet latter days, was on the whole content with her achievement. If the experiment had shown at what points personal freedom dashes itself against insuperable barriers, it was something gained to have those limits roughly mapped. People – especially women – have certainly been the freer because one immensely courageous and highly vocal woman explored the uncleared country for them.

'We artists,' she wrote to Flaubert, 'have no patience. We want the Abbey of Thelema at once; but, before saying "Do what you want!" one must go through with, "Do what you can."' She, at least, had done what she could.

ACKNOWLEDGMENTS

In Section V, quotations from the translations of *Letters of George Sand*, published by Routledge, are on pages 207–8; from the translation of George Sand's *Intimate Journal*, published by Williams and Norgate, on page 198, lines 8–11, pages 199, 205–6, 206, lines 13–15, and line 31 to page 207, line 4; from the translation of the *George Sand – Gustave Flaubert Letters*, published by Duckworth, on pages 210, 214, 215. Quotations on page 176, line 25, page 185, lines 1–22, page 203, lines 2–4, and page 210, lines 26–31, are from translations given in *George Sand and her Lovers*, by Francis Gribble, whose epigram on George Sand is also quoted on page 214; the publishers are Grayson and Grayson.

In Section V the quotations on pages 178, 179, 180, 188, 194 (lines 10–14), 205 (lines 14–16), 206 (lines 16–20 and 23–27), are from *Letters of George Sand*, published by Ward and Downey. Other translations in this Section are original.

Ugr
CT
105
J3
1970

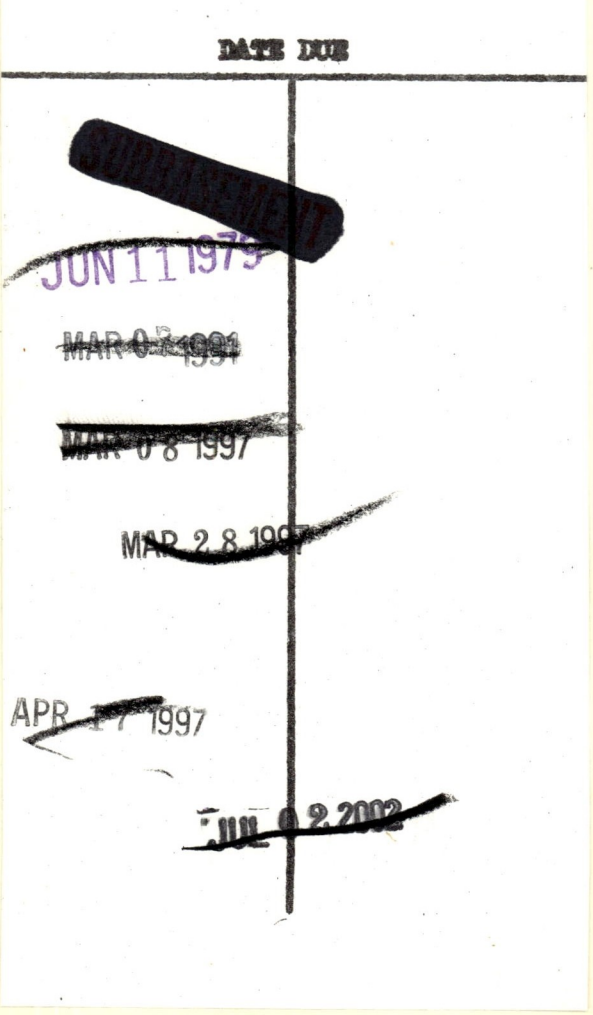